the
inbetweeners
A-Z

the
inbetweeners
A-Z

**MATTHEW RICHARDSON
AND MIKE DODGSON**

JOHN BLAKE

Published by John Blake Publishing Ltd,
3 Bramber Court, 2 Bramber Road,
London W14 9PB, England

www.johnblakepublishing.co.uk

www.facebook.com/Johnblakepub facebook
twitter.com/johnblakepub twitter

First published in paperback in 2011

ISBN: 978 1 84358 355 4

British Library Cataloguing-in-Publication Data:

A catalogue record for this book is available from the British Library.

Design by www.envydesign.co.uk

Printed and bound by CPI Group (UK) Ltd, Croydon, CR0 4YY

3 5 7 9 10 8 6 4 2

Papers used by John Blake Publishing are natural, recyclable products made
from wood grown in sustainable forests. The manufacturing processes
conform to the environmental regulations of the country of origin.

Dedications

Matthew: Dedicated to the three women in my life: Katie, Mum and Olivia.

Mike: For my mum and dad (sorry about the language!)

The Inbetweeners A–Z is packed full of everything you need to know about the award-winning British comedy. Read all about the show's characters, actors, filming locations and how it was made. Find out what inspirations the writers had to make the series and how they eventually picked the actors to play the awesome foursome: Will, Simon, Neil and Jay.

This book contains all your favourite quotes and comedy moments from the hit TV show, including Bus Wankers, the tramp's shoes and the legendary fashion show. Plus, get a full breakdown of every episode from Series One, Two and Three with the best bits, lots of facts and the funniest quotes.

Find out what the cast and crew were tweeting while making the movie; also how they prepared for it and discover how fans were given the chance to join in.

With this A–Z guide, you can even learn how to speak like an Inbetweener with a full glossary of the show's filthiest, funniest words and catchphrases!

Authors Mike Dodgson and Matthew Richardson are

addicted to *The Inbetweeners*. They've compiled everything an *Inbetweeners'* fan could ever want to know in this A–Z guide.

You can read this book from start to finish, or dip in and out of it, if you prefer. ENJOY!

a is for...

Alan Cooper

Alan is the frisky father of Inbetweener Simon. He appears in ten episodes throughout the three series. There's nothing the 40ish-year-old loves more than embarrassing his sexually frustrated son. When Si and his mates actually manage to get invited to a party (or at least to sneak into one), Alan is always on hand to give them a lift home.

On the outside, Alan seems like every other run-of-the-mill father but beneath his responsible exterior lurks the libido of a sexually frustrated teenager and there's nothing he loves more than revealing saucy details about his and Mrs Cooper's goings-on to their son. Although Simon hates his dad's stories, the other Inbetweeners love them – and we do too!

FUNNIEST SCENE

Alan Cooper's funniest scene is when he hands over the keys to Simon's Fiat Cinquecento Hawaii edition, as congratulations for passing his driving test. Simon is appalled at how shit the car is, but Alan plays it cool, just happy that it's too rubbish for his son to be able to speed in.

LOVES

White suits with grass stains
Talking to Simon about his sexual encounters

HATES

Simon's bad language
Buying his son a car… only for it to be ruined on the first day!

HOBBIES

When Alan's not driving Simon and his mates around, he can usually be found canoodling with his wife Pamela.

Did you know?
There's an ongoing joke across the three series of the show that, when Simon swears in front of Alan or Pamela, they almost always give him a polite reminder to watch what he's saying – 'language!' – although it never seems to work.

Alistair Scott

Alistair appears in the first episode of Series Three; he is a student at Rudge Park Comprehensive, who puts on a fashion show to raise money and awareness for his kidney-failure condition, which has left him wheelchair-bound. Most of Rudge Park's pupils have rallied round to support this more-than-worthy cause, although Alistair is disliked by the four Inbetweeners due to his short temper and attitude. Alistair is played by English actor Steven Webb, a child star who since the age of ten has appeared in many theatre productions and TV shows; his major TV work includes *The Magician's House*, *Holby City*, *Bad Girls* and *Doctors*. In his other work, Steven appeared as a dancer in the now infamous Michael Jackson performance at the Brit Awards in 1996, when Jarvis Cocker ran on to the stage. Apparently, Webb cracked a rib when Cocker accidentally ran into him on the stage.

Andrew Cooper

Andrew is Inbetweener Simon's younger brother and represents pretty much all little brothers around the country; he is the scourge of Simon's privacy and takes every opportunity to embarrass him in front of his friends and girlfriends, often outwitting him. A prime example of this is during the 'Bunk Off' episode when Andrew begins to tell Simon in front of his friends how the whole school was laughing about him painting 'I love Carli D'Amato' on her driveway: 'He's made you look a right knob' was the comment from Jay. Andrew appears in six episodes altogether throughout the series, often with only a small part.

Andrew Cooper is played by actor Dominic Applewhite. Before appearing in *The Inbetweeners*, Dominic had one acting credit to his name in the children's TV series *M.I. High*. After being cast in all three series of *The Inbetweeners*, he then had a small role in the multi-award-winning film *The King's Speech* as the speech therapist Lionel Logue's son, Valentine. In 2011, *The King's Speech* received numerous awards and, after being nominated for 12 awards at the Oscars, the British film went on to win Best Picture and Best Director, and Colin Firth took the award for Best Actor for his portrayal of King George VI.

Did you know?

Dominic Applewhite, the actor who plays Andrew Cooper, grew over a foot in height across the course of the three series. As he's not a featured character in the series, his size is apparent when comparing the first series to the third. His growth spurt was so obvious that, in one of his final scenes on the show, Dominic had to sit on a smaller stool than his co-star Joe Thomas, so he still looked like his 'little' brother.

GOING STATESIDE. ZACK PEARLMAN AND BUBBA LEWIS ARE TWO OF THE ACTORS WHO WILL APPEAR IN THE US INBETWEENERS SERIES.

Around the World

The Inbetweeners has made an impact not only in the UK, but also on international audiences – and it's not just Jay's awful Aussie impressions as 'Bret Clement' that have done the trick. 'Three jars of lager and a pint of Guinness' hardly makes him a Rolf Harris sound-alike, but *The Inbetweeners* has made it in Australia since the show first began to air in 2010. It's also been broadcast in the US: on BBC America and MTV Latin America.

In fact, *The Inbetweeners* has made such noise across the pond that MTV has commissioned a full season of a US version of the show. *Entertainment Weekly* reported that MTV are to make 12 episodes of the sitcom starring Bubba Lewis, Joey Pollari, Zack Pearlman and Mark L. Young as the four awkward teenagers at the centre of the show.

David Janollari, MTV's executive vice president in charge of scripted development, told *Deadline*, '*The Inbetweeners* is one of the best comedies to come out of the UK in years.'

Eager to make the show a success, MTV have brought in some big guns to look over the project. Brad Copeland and Aaron Kaplan will exec-produce the series, alongside Iain Morris and Damon Beesley, original creators of the show.

Copeland's credits as a producer and writer include big US TV shows such as *Arrested Development* and *My Name*

Is Earl. He has also written for several film productions including *Wild Hogs* (2007) starring Tim Allen, John Travolta, Martin Lawrence and William H. Macy.

Kaplan's credits include exec-producing on *Made of Honor* (2008) and *You, Me and Dupree* (2006) starring Owen Wilson.

The four actors signed up to play the US *Inbetweeners* are more experienced in the world of TV and film than the UK originals were when they first started. Although none of them has 'made it big' as yet, they will all be familiar faces to the US audience.

Before being signed up for the US version of the show, Lewis played guest roles in episodes of *Numb3rs* and *Grey's Anatomy*, as well as appearing in several TV movies. Co-star Pollari is best known in the US for his roles in Disney films *Skyrunners* (2009) and *Avalon High* (2010).

Young has made numerous one-off TV appearances, including episodes of *Dexter*, *Criminal Minds* and *CSI:NY*, having also had the recurring role of 'Franky' in the third season of HBO's *Big Love*.

Pearlman's résumé best resembles that of an 'original Inbetweener', thanks to his role in 2010 comedy *The Virginity Hit*, produced by Will Ferrell and *Anchorman* director Adam McKay. The movie follows the journey of a gang of four teenagers embarking on sex for the first time (sounds familiar?!).

Despite having some experience in the TV world, it's still a massive opportunity for all four guys, something that can be seen through some of their Twitter accounts. Pollari replying to a retweet on the story: 'Ridiculously pumped for this. Can't wait to start', while Pearlman tweeted his thanks to the show's original co-creator Iain Morris: 'You just made me blush! Thanks for creating such an amazing show and letting us shit on it. Move to the US, we have donuts!'

Did you know?
'Bret Clement', the name used for Jay's fake Australian ID in the first episode of the UK series, was a nod of recognition by the show's writers Beesley and Morris to Bret McKenzie and Jemaine Clement, writers of the hit New Zealand comedy *Flight of the Conchords*.

Awards

The Inbetweeners has been nominated for and won numerous awards since going on-air. After the first series, the show won Best New TV Comedy and Best Male Comedy Newcomer (Simon Bird – for the role of Will) at the British Comedy Awards 2008. The raucous nature of the awards ceremony became

THE CAST CELEBRATE WINING THE DIGITAL CHOICE AWARD AT THE NATIONAL TELEVISION AWARDS IN 2011.

apparent when members of the cast and crew were greeted onstage by a barrage of missiles such as bottles and tableware from fellow comedy actors, with Kevin Bishop being the ringleader. At the same event, during Simon Bird's acceptance speech for Best Male Comedy Newcomer, he dedicated his award to the writers of the show and his fellow Inbetweeners. 2008 also saw the show win Best New British TV Sitcom at the Comedy.co.uk awards.

The following year, *The Inbetweeners* won Best Comedy Show at the TV Choice Awards, an annual awards ceremony where all of the gongs are presented on the basis of votes cast by readers of magazines *TV Choice* and *TV Quick*. In 2009 and 2010, the British Academy Television Awards, otherwise known as the BAFTAs, nominated the show for Best Situation Comedy, and in 2010 at the same event, the sitcom was presented with the YouTube Audience Award. While accepting the award, the writers Damon Beesley and Iain Morris dedicated it to all of their friends growing up who inspired the stories in the show. The final award the show won in 2010 was Best Situation Comedy at the prestigious Rose d'Or Festival, an international entertainment awards festival set in Lucerne, Switzerland.

In 2011, *The Inbetweeners* won Best Sitcom at the British Comedy Awards, as well as the Digital Choice Award at the National Television Awards, based on votes from the general public. Thankfully, the show beat off competition from *Glee* and *Peter Andre: The Next Chapter*!

b is for...

Ben Palmer

British writer, producer and director Ben Palmer has worked on many Channel 4 TV and film projects and, in 2011, he directed *The Inbetweeners'* film.

Palmer seemed the perfect choice for the film, having directed all 12 episodes of Series Two and Three. He has a vast amount of experience in directing many of Britain's best-loved comedies. In 2004, he co-wrote and produced *A Bear's Christmas Tail*, a TV film comedy following a well-spoken but potty-mouthed bear from the mind of Leigh Francis, the performer who also brought us 'Avid Merrion' and 'Keith Lemon'. During the next few years, Palmer stuck with Francis to co-write and direct much of *Bo Selecta, Bo in the USA* and *Keith Lemon's Very Brilliant World Tour.*

In 2008, his directing resumé continued on *Star Stories*, a Channel 4 comedy series parodying the lives of celebrities such as Bono, Kate Moss and Elton John. After he directed Series Two and Three of *The Inbetweeners*, in 2010 the show received a nomination for Best Situation Comedy at the BAFTA TV awards.

Sandwiched between the second and third series of *The Inbetweeners*, Palmer directed two episodes of the TV series *Comedy Lab*, a series of shows and sketches from various writers and producers. The second of these episodes starred actor James Buckley, who plays Jay in *The Inbetweeners*.

In 2011, Palmer was due to direct the comedy series *Sex and the Chippy* until he was offered the chance to direct *The Inbetweeners'* film. Eventually, British comedy legend Harry Enfield stood in for Palmer.

BIEBER FEVER

Teen-pop sensation Justin Bieber has revealed that he's a massive fan of *The Inbetweeners*. He told the *Mirror* that he 'came across *The Inbetweeners* and, man, it was the funniest thing I had ever seen'.

The teen heartthrob even volunteered to take time out of his busy schedule to make a cameo appearance

Justin Bieber would love to make a cameo appearance in The Inbetweeners.

in the show, if he was ever wanted: 'So many high school shows try to glamorise school, but this was real and that's what made it so funny. If they are going to make a fourth series or a movie, I would make sure I was free to do a cameo. If they want me, I'm there.'

Although it sounds like Bieber would love to be involved in the show, his boyish good looks and millions of dollars may make him stand out from Jay, Simon, Neil and Will!

And he's not the only celebrity fan to have shown an interest in making a special appearance. It was reported that Amanda Holden also wanted to make a guest cameo in the series, along with some of football's biggest

JOE THOMAS REPORTED THAT SIMON COWELL WAS LESS THAN IMPRESSED WHEN THE INBETWEENERS BEAT BRITAIN'S GOT TALENT TO THE BAFTA YOUTUBE AUDIENCE AWARD!

names. Blake Harrison (Neil) and Simon Bird (Will) told the *Daily Star*, 'Apparently, Wayne Rooney and Rio Ferdinand want parts in the show. And Amanda Holden told us she wants to play a sexy English teacher in the next series.'

It's hard to imagine Ferdinand and Rooney playing for Rudge Park Comp's school football team, with Holden heading up the English department. Surely even Gilbert would have cracked a smile at that one!

Did you know?

The Inbetweeners beat *Britain's Got Talent* to the BAFTA YouTube Audience Award. Joe Thomas told the *Daily Star* that head of the show Simon Cowell looked less than impressed when the winners were announced: 'Simon pulled a face. It was like, "Damn those pesky school kids for ruining my plans!" Everyone said he was joking but I'm not so sure.'

Big John

REPORT CARD

Food Technology: A+ – John is clearly passionate about food and this shows all the time! If he's not eating the stuff, he's talking about it.

Psychology: F – John's experiences with a shrink have made him weary around other people.

Sex Education: F – John showed some promise in this area at a recent Saturday-night house party but has since floundered.

Business Studies: B – John's running of the food stand at the Xmas Prom showed real business nous. Maybe he should consider a career in the catering industry.

BACKGROUND

Big John is introduced in the first episode of *The Inbetweeners*. A victim of bullying in his previous school, John joins Will and the other 'freaks' on their first day, hoping to make a fresh start. Unfortunately for him, however, any hopes of a new beginning don't pan out and, once again, he ends up often being the butt of the joke. Despite his unpopularity at Rudge Park, Simon Bird (Will) revealed Big John is his favourite character in an E4 web chat with fans.

Big John does have some happier times in the show. When Neil, Jay, Simon and Will attempt to get into a house party after Will's birthday dinner party was a flop, they look through the window to see John engaged in deep conversation while resting his hand on a girl's breast! And his luck with the ladies spurs the lads on to climb over a garden fence just to get into the party.

At the Rudge Park Xmas Prom, John tells Jay that he has been seeing a counsellor. Although it's not revealed why, this is one of the few times in the show where we see a more honest side to Jay, as he opens up to John, explaining that his often ludicrous tales are just his way of getting noticed.

FUNNIEST SCENE

When John helps Will to organise the Xmas Prom, he takes charge of organising the food for the event. This is the biggest-speaking part Big John has, showing his passion for everything related to food. Later, he is caught eating the burgers he's meant to be handing out.

LOVES

Eating two yoghurts at once
Lasagne
Burgers

HATES
Bullies

HOBBIES
There's nothing John loves more than eating, whether it's two yoghurts at once or burger after burger... after burger.

> *Did you know?*
> The actor John Seaward who plays Big John was at the original auditions for the pilot. On a recall audition, he told the commissioning editor Caroline Leddy (responsible for commissioning shows including *Trigger Happy TV*, *Green Wing* and *The IT Crowd*) that he couldn't believe they'd asked him back as he thought he was rubbish on his first audition! Obviously, the production team didn't think so, and writers Beesley and Morris revealed they wrote the part for John to play.

Blake Harrison

Half-wit Neil Sutherland is played by the actor Blake Harrison. Born on 23 July 1985, in Peckham, South London, he joined the performing arts establishment The BRIT School at the age of 14. The London school provides a platform for aspiring young actors, performers

BLAKE HARRISON PLAYS HALF-WIT NEIL SUTHERLAND.

and media producers. It boasts an impressive list of former pupils including Adele, Katie Melua, Leona Lewis and Emily Head (who plays Carli), Blake's co-star in *The Inbetweeners*.

After leaving The BRIT School, Blake featured in a few low-key productions before appearing in two episodes of *The Bill* in 2008, playing the character of Pete Monks. In the same year, he auditioned for *The Inbetweeners*, while working in a Carphone Warehouse store. After landing the part of Neil, and following three extremely successful series, he acquired the nickname 'one-take Blake' from his fellow actors due to his incredibly professional attitude on set.

In 2010, Blake had the enviable job of many men when he worked with glamour model Keeley Hazell and a host of other scantily clad models for an online Lynx film, 'Keeping Keeley'. The short follows his character Jack as he aims to maintain the attention of Miss Hazell and asks the viewer to make decisions as he 'twists' his appearance.

After finishing the final series of *The Inbetweeners* (which aired in the autumn of 2010), Blake played Barney in a single episode of the BBC3 comedy *Him & Her*, about a young couple and written by writer and performer Stefan Golaszewski. After *Him & Her*, he starred in Channel 4's *The Increasingly Poor Decisions of Todd Margaret* as 'Dave' – a sitcom about an American who bluffs his way into a sales job with his only employee played by Blake. *Todd Margaret* was written by David Cross and Shaun Pye. Cross is an American writer and performer famous for playing Tobias in the critically acclaimed *Arrested Development*, while Pye is an English writer, actor and critic, who has written for many British TV shows and also played Greg in *Extras* alongside Ricky Gervais and Stephen Merchant. Both *Him & Her* and *The Increasingly Poor Decisions of Todd Margaret* were successful in the debuts and commissioned for a second series in late 2010 and early 2011, respectively. In 2011, Blake starred in an episode of the BBC comedy *White Van Man*, about Ollie (played by former *Hollyoaks* star Will Mellor) and his painting and decorating business.

Away from filming, he is a massive Millwall FC fan and also an avid user of the social network site Twitter, where he was sending updates on filming *The Inbetweeners'* movie to his 28,000-plus followers. In one tweet, it seemed Blake had become very frustrated at photographers while filming on location: 'real shame paps keep getting shots of good moments of the film. Unfortunately the main people that lose out are fans that won't be surprised'. Towards the end of March 2011, he also toasted the end of filming *The Inbetweeners'* movie: 'Filming done! It's sad but no time to wallow as drinking is afoot! This way to the finest tankards of ale Magaluf has to offer!'

Did you know?
Originally James Buckley (who plays Jay Cartwright in the series) auditioned for the role of Neil and it wasn't until the producers saw Blake play the part that they decided to go for him instead.

BLAKE HARRISON ATTENDED THE BRIT SCHOOL FOR THE PERFORMING ARTS FROM THE AGE OF 14.

Bumder

The word 'Bumder' comes from Episode Two of Series One – the 'Bunk Off' episode, where the lads decide to skip school to drink gin and Drambuie. According to Will, a 'Bumder' is a mixture of bummer and bender, and the derogatory term was used as an insult to Neil's 'gay' dad when he catches them bunking off at Neil's house.

Although Will regretted the incident afterwards, it seemed to gain him instant respect from both Simon and Jay.

'Bunk Off': Series One, Episode Two

Bunking off is a time-honoured tradition around the world and it's no different for *The Inbetweeners'* characters.

The second episode of Series One – 'Bunk Off' – starts off with Will and the other Inbetweeners playing Frisbee, as Will's idea of a way to get girls (no wonder he doesn't have much luck in that department!). So, to impress Carli D'Amato and her friends, he throws the Frisbee their way and in a completely uncoordinated, but hilarious moment ends up landing it right in the face of a wheelchair-bound girl.

Neil and Jay quickly leg it, with Will and Simon following closely behind. When the panic is over, the four decide to go ahead with their plan of bunking off the next day. This is unlike Will and a big change in character: fresh out of private school following his parents' break-up, he is reluctant to join the other three truants, but the next morning he heads over to Simon's house to start their day of freedom.

After Simon and Will manage to convince Simon's mum that there's a sixth form-only non-uniform day, Si decides the next step in the plan is to call the school secretary to let her know that he and Will won't be attending that day. He rings and attempts an atrocious impression of his mum, sounding more like a boy going through puberty than a middle-aged woman. Still, the secretary seems fooled and decides to pass him on to Mr Gilbert, head of sixth form, who is wise to Simon's terrible impersonation of his mum: 'OK, Simon, that's enough! I know you're bullshitting me. Get in before you make things worse for yourself.' Ignoring Gilbert's warning, and after Will describes the attempt as 'fucking awful', Simon convinces himself that he's pulled it off and the pair decide to go through with bunking off for the day.

Next on the agenda is booze. This time it's Will who hatches a 'brilliant' plan and, to make sure they get served, he decides to don Simon's dad's suit and his own, very unstylish hat. The only problem is that, rather than looking like a refined, mature businessman, Will admits to looking more like a 'Hasidic Jew'.

Despite his 'stylish' attire and chat with the shopkeeper, explaining that he's recently moved into the area and is planning a housewarming party, no one's going to be fooled that Will is over eighteen. However, along with the party-size packets of crisps he takes to the counter, the shopkeeper serves him two bottles of gin and a bottle of whisky liquor, just to get him out the store.

This isn't exactly the cans of lager the boys had planned, and, after giving Will some stick for his choice of booze and the fact that he actually bought crisps, the gang decide to go to Neil's, where he's promised to show them his dad's porn collection to prove he's not gay!

Back at Neil's, and after they've each knocked back a few shots of gin, the alcohol begins to take effect and revelations start to pour out. Neil admits his plans to pleasure himself over thoughts of Will's fit mum, Simon declares his love for classmate Carli (although everyone knew anyway), and Jay claims the regular caravan holidays he goes on with his family are basically massive orgies. Then, as Jay is riding Simon and singing a song about Carli's fanny, Neil's dad walks in with 'Mr Chippy', Kevin Sutherland's local friendly tradesman.

Not used to alcohol, Will is feeling the effects more than anyone, so, rather than being his usual polite and respectful self that parents love, he takes the opportunity to have a hilarious rant at Neil's tank-top-wearing dad when he expresses his disappointment of their behaviour, 'I've had enough of your lip,' to which Will replies, 'Oh, you'd like my lip, wouldn't you, right round your bell-end... You BUMDER!' Even foul-mouthed Jay is shocked at Will's new mean streak.

After being thrown out, it's Simon's turn for a bright idea. Therefore, it's off to Carli's so he can express his love for her. However, rather than a text or a phone call, he decides a grand gesture is needed and spraypaints 'I love Carli D'Amato' on her driveway!

Carli is less than impressed at Si's antics, but, to help save an ounce of his dignity and his complete embarrassment in front of Jay and Neil, she invites him round to the house later that evening when she's babysitting her younger brother, Chris. Jay reckons Carli's 'gagging for it' and that she loves it that Simon's hammered, and so convinces Si to continue drinking for the rest of the day. Of course, this results in Simon turning up to Carli's house later that night absolutely wasted.

Unsurprisingly, things don't go quite as planned, with the drink really taking its toll on Simon. He ends up vomiting everywhere, including in Chris's face! This leaves Si one step further from any chance of a relationship with Carli. The episode ends with Will and Simon's parents all laughing at how pathetic their teenage sons are!

Did you know?

When Simon spraypaints on Carli's driveway, you only see him adding the last letter of her surname. Her first name is actually spelled wrong – 'Carly', not 'Carli' as it should be. Definitely one for the bloopers reel, not to mention the continuity!

In addition, this episode was inspired by the experiences of the writers, who recalled dressing up in their parents' clothes and buying crisps to try to get served – at least Will's not the only one!

OPPOSITE: WILL SIMON EVER WIN THE HEART OF CARLI? PROBABLY NOT BY VOMITING ON HER YOUNGER BROTHER!

C is for...

'Camping': Series Three, Episode Six

The final episode of Series Three starts with Inbetweener Simon finding out in an emergency family meeting that he and his family have to move to Swansea, Wales, for his dad to keep his job. After finding out where Swansea actually is, Si is shocked by the news as you might expect, but his rant is a bit of an overreaction culminating in a refusal to go: 'I'm not going. How's that suit your fucking plans?!'

Back at school, Si explains his situation to the other Inbetweeners, but Jay and Neil in their usual, unsympathetic manner see this as their opportunity to 'have a crack' at Carli D'Amato. This is the scene where Neil reveals some BIG news of his own. He tells the gang that, following a sexual encounter with 'saucy ASDA Karen' at work, where she seduced him over the cheese counter, he thinks he's going to become a dad after she texted him: 'Did the test. It's positive. Thought you should know:/'.

Will recommends that Neil talks to Mr Gilbert about the prospect of him entering fatherhood, but Gilbert in his usual unhelpful manner says that, so long as it didn't happen at school or with a pupil, he doesn't care: 'That Sutherland's managed to pass his genes on may be a looming disaster for mankind, but it is not my mess to clean up!'

When Simon bumps into Carli, she tells him she has heard about the news of him moving away. She explains how disappointed she is and that she always thought at some point they might… but, before the immortal words cross her lips, she's dragged away by her friend Rachel. However, this is the biggest indication Simon has ever had that she likes him and, finishing her sentence in an act of desperation, he shouts 'make love' across the canteen!

To cheer Simon up, Will decides that a camping trip is just what the lads need. But Neil's the only one who fancies the trip: Jay explains how last time he went to the country he had some trouble with cows, which ended with them standing up and 'spraying milk from their tits', while Simon just wants to use his last two weeks before the move to get Carli.

At 2am the next morning, a drunken Simon calls Will to tell him he's hatched a plan to impress the love of his life. This isn't the first time alcohol has affected Si's judgement around Carli, so Will goes to meet him (dressing gown and slippers included). He catches Simon on the roof of Carli's house climbing into a bedroom window. What Simon doesn't know is that this is her younger brother's bedroom and, as he climbs on to the bed to wake Carli up, after again declaring his love, little Chris D'Amato wakes up and screams for his dad. Simon makes a very quick exit!

This is the turning point for Simon and he decides that maybe a camping trip isn't the worst thing he could do. So, Monopoly on board, the four head off to a secluded lake and woodlands in Simon's shitty yellow car. The first topic of conversation on their arrival is the toilet situation. Neil reveals he's already desperate for a number two and that he gets emotional when he needs to go. Will's scouting experience comes into play and he breaks the news to the others that they'll have to rough it and each dig a trench. This is too much for the suburban kids and they decide it's back to the pub they passed on the way to take a dump before they even think about camping.

When they return from their toilet duties, Will makes the mistake of leaving the others unattended. In his absence, Jay decides to get the fire going and, despite Will's earlier warning that 'Fire is an element – it must be respected', Jay decides to build one with petrol, Will's fold-up table and his picnic basket!

When Will returns, he goes absolutely mental at Jay, understandably opening up into an epic rant. To lighten the mood and cheer Will up, Jay suggests a campfire game but, instead of toasting marshmallows and telling ghost stories, the Inbetweeners decide to each swap phones and send one message to anyone in each of their phonebooks. The only rules of the game are that you can write anything you want on the other person's phone, send it to anyone you choose and there's nothing they can do to stop you. Jay's first up and he decides to send Carli a message from Simon, declaring his love for her in his usual filthy way. Will's up next and he texts Jay's dad, telling him he's thinking about him in the bath and is 'hard'. Neil does the predictable and informs Will's mum that 'it's been seventeen years, and I'd love to have another go on your big old tits'. But the best of the four is Simon texting 'saucy ASDA Karen' from Neil, asking her to marry him, following Neil's revelation that he's going to be a dad.

The guys quickly start to realise that, even with Jay's texting game, camping isn't all Will had made it out to be.

As a last resort, they agree to a game of Monopoly, much to Will's delight – that is, until he finds out Jay's actually rather good. Using the darkness as an excuse to 'call it a draw', Will tries to end the game, but Jay, being determined to win, refuses to give up and moves Si's car in a position to light up the campsite with the headlights. But Jay forgets to put the handbrake on, with the keys left in the car. The four end up in front of the shit mobile, trying to stop it from rolling into the lake. As Simon and Will look for something to smash the window, Jay and Neil decide it's inevitable that the vehicle is going into the lake and agree to let it roll. This leaves Simon absolutely distraught, his car in the lake, his clothes soaking wet and his last chance to get off with Carli spent in a tent with three idiots!

When Si calms down, the four make a hasty retreat to the tent, where the texts come back from the earlier game. Neil is overjoyed to find out it wasn't a child that Karen was bearing, but instead she had Chlamydia. Jay's dad tells him they knew he should have seen a shrink, while Will's mum passes right over the 'tits' comment and tells him she loves him. Simon doesn't show the others his text back from Carli, but his smile suggests it's good news.

The night ends in a disgusting mess, with Neil throwing up all over Will's head (thanks to under-cooked sausages), leading Simon and Jay to throw up, too! So

SIMON BIRD (WILL), EMILY HEAD (CARLI), JOE THOMAS (SIMON) AND BLAKE HARRISON (NEIL) AT THE BRITISH COMEDY AWARDS.

they're all left walking home, covered in sick – Simon couldn't have hoped for a better send-off!

'Caravan Club': Series One, Episode Five

The 'Caravan Club' sees the foursome take a trip to the famous Camber Sands. With Simon, Will and Neil at a loose end for the weekend, Jay declares he'll be 'up to his nuts in guts' and they should all come along to experience it. Not thinking for one second they would all agree, Jay's bluff is called and so they set off on the motorway to the caravan site with the 'Special Edition' Cinquecento topping an unprecedented 100mph on the way!

While they are checking out the 'clunge mags' at the service station, the dulcet tones of Leona Lewis reveal there is a text message for Simon from Becky (one of the girls at the Caravan Club) – Jay had told her that the lads were on their way and up for meeting up. With the prospect of getting laid at the unlikeliest of venues, the weekend was looking up: 'First rule of Caravan Club is that everyone gets some!'

As they pull into the caravan park, there doesn't seem to be much action around until they bump into Becky and her sister, and after a brief exchange of words they agree to meet up again at the party later that evening.

This episode is the first time we meet Jay's dad and

he announces himself with some distaste while on the toilet as the boys eat dinner in the family caravan. The stench is enough to put anyone off their food, so they start getting ready for the big party.

As the lacklustre event gets under way, they start to wonder why they're standing in the middle of a barn watching an old woman dance with an eight-year-old, that is until Neil busts the robotic moves and, more importantly, Becky – Simon's 'ride for the evening' – turns up with a friend. As Jay starts to convince him that Becky is definitely up for it, the night at Camber Sands Caravan Club begins to get interesting for it seems it isn't only Simon who is about to get lucky. However, after being propositioned by a young lady, Will appears more interested in eating hummus and skidding in his socks on the dance floor: 'Come on, let's skid!'

As Will's night deteriorates in some style, Simon enjoys a slow dance and a spot of heavy petting with Becky to 'Careless Whisper' by George Michael. They agree to go outside and, with Jay's approval and the promise to fill up a Durex on the way out, the couple are out the door. The heavy petting continues outside the party barn and, with Becky's back turned, Simon's pants are well and truly round his ankles! 'What the hell are you doing?' screams the distraught Becky, and the response from Simon well and truly humiliates the pair of them: 'It's a condom – I thought we should be safe!' Unfortunately, Jay's bullshit has yet again worked wonders and the pair go their separate ways, wires definitely crossed!

The weekend wasn't a complete disaster, though: apparently one of the foursome did get lucky at Caravan Club. On the way home from Camber Sands, the seats of the Cinquecento feel a little damp, at which point Neil declares he had a rendezvous with the girl Will turned down for skids and hummus. If anything good was to come of the weekend, it was that the bright-yellow Fiat had developed a new nickname: 'the spunk mobile'.

Carli D'Amato

REPORT CARD

Sociology: A+ – Thanks to Simon's help, revising in his room.

Geography: A+ – Again, thanks to Simon... who doesn't even take the subject!

Fashion: B – Would have got an A if it wasn't for the balls-up at the end of the fashion show.

Psychology: C – Good at stringing Simon along, but lets her guard down in the end.

Art: E – Her likening of Simon's graffiti to Banksy let her down here.

CARLI D'AMATO IS PLAYED BY ACTRESS EMILY HEAD.

BACKGROUND

Carli D'Amato is Simon's love interest in the series; however, for the majority of the show, she doesn't seem to display much interest and only really sees him as a close family friend. In turn, Simon doesn't do much to endear himself to Carli, as every time they meet, in or out of school, he manages to say something completely ridiculous to make a complete arse of himself. Simon's friends don't really chat with Carli during the series and somehow feel she is leading him on: this seems evident in the 'Bunk Off' episode when she invites him round after he spraypaints 'I love Carli D'Amato' on the driveway of her house. The invitation appears to be one of fondness; however, on the surface she only really invites him round to spite his mocking friends.

Carli has an on-off relationship with Tom, an older and burly, rugby-playing type, who is the scourge of Simon's advances. At the end of the second series, Carli asks if she can revise at Simon's house, where they share a kiss and, after agreeing to meet in the pub later that evening, Simon gives her a mix tape with songs that explain the way he is feeling. Unfortunately for Si, she knocks him back again when Tom appears to spoil the party.

Carli's friends include Rachel, a girl she went clubbing with during the London episode. While in the club, Carli and Rachel meet a group of friends and, once again, Simon humiliates himself trying to win her affections while wearing a pair of tramp's shoes covered in urine.

Simon and Carli's relationship takes a hit at the start of the third series when she feels he has embarrassed her by mistakenly getting his testicle out while parading on the catwalk of the fashion show. However, when she finds out that he will be leaving for Swansea at the end of the same series, Carli starts to show her true feelings for Simon before being interrupted. While Simon is on the camping trip with the rest of his group, she texts him something that is never revealed.

Carli lives with her parents and her little brother Chris. Her mum and dad are mentioned on a handful of occasions; however, Mr D'Amato never appears in the show and Mrs D'Amato only makes a brief appearance. Chris D'Amato is seen in the 'Bunk Off' episode when Simon throws up on his head and, once again, in the final episode of the third series after Simon breaks into the house and is accused of touching him in bed.

FUNNIEST SCENE

Carli's funniest scene has to be when she asks Simon if she can revise at his house because they have currently got the builders in. Simon mistakes this for a euphemism and asks if this is the same as 'having the painters in'. The cringeworthy scene is another example of the humiliation that Simon puts himself through in front of Carli.

LOVES
Her boyfriend Tom
Playing with Simon's head
London clubbing

HATES
Her boyfriend Tom
Simon calling her 'babes'
People trying to ruin the fashion show
Simon throwing up in her little brother's face

HOBBIES
Carli is very sociable and loves going to the pub with friends, spending the night clubbing in London and a walk in the park with the girls.

> *Did you know?*
> When Carli sent a text to Simon at the end of the final episode, the writers were so secretive that even the actress who plays Carli, Emily Head, didn't know the content of the message. The secrecy left everyone guessing that their love story would be wrapped up in the 2011 film.

FINDING THE PERFECT ACTORS TO PLAY
THE BOYS HAS BEEN KEY TO THE MASSIVE
SUCCESS OF THE SHOW.

Casting

The writers of *The Inbetweeners*, Damon Beesley and Iain Morris, knew that getting the perfect cast was key to making the show a success. So, in the hunt for the right actors, thousands of boys were auditioned for the parts of Will McKenzie, Simon Cooper, Neil Sutherland and Jay Cartwright.

Iain Morris describes the show as 'a slice of life a lot of people would relate to. It's about being normal at school, rather than particularly fantastically cool and exciting.' This is what made it so important for them to get the main characters exactly how they'd imagined. They couldn't be too cool, too good-looking or too geeky; they had to be just in the middle – they really needed to find Inbetweeners.

Joe Thomas (Simon) and Simon Bird (Will) were actually known to the writers from the start of the project but at first they didn't feel they were right for the show. It was only when the pair saw Thomas and Bird's sketch act for the Edinburgh Comedy Festival in 2007 that they changed their minds.

James Buckley (Jay) was originally cast as Neil, with the writers later deciding he'd be better as Jay, while Blake was fresh out of drama college when he took on the role. It was all coming together and the vision of the writers worked with the four main characters.

Iain Morris revealed that Henry Lloyd-Hughes, the

actor who plays Mark Donovan, was originally discounted for the role on the grounds of being too posh. The actor managed to change the mind of the show's creators when he came to an audition already acting the part of the school bully, though. He entered with his swagger on, wearing a necklace with a gun symbol, and talking about his rough life in Hackney. Thanks to this great piece of method acting, Lloyd-Hughes was hired.

Despite the best efforts of the show's makers to find the perfect cast, Blake Harrison's (Neil) cast interviews paint a less-than-perfect picture. During filming for the first series, Harrison seized the chance to get the low-down on some of the main characters and so he took a video camera to interview the cast of the show, asking them to vote on some hot topics. Here are some of his best questions:

- Who's the cleverest? – Simon 'Cambridge University' Bird
- Who's the dumbest? – Every cast member agreed on James Buckley
- Who's the most professional? – Blake 'One-take Blake' Harrison
- Who moans the most? – James Buckley
- Who has the worst habits? – Joe was voted to have the worst habits.

Thankfully, Blake's questions didn't rule out any of the guys when it comes to being hilarious and brilliant actors!

Charlotte 'Big Jugs' Hinchcliffe

REPORT CARD

Sex Education: A+ – Charlotte's favourite subject by far: she has perfect attendance and has excelled with the homework! It's rumoured she's continued her studies at university.

Biology: A+ – Excellent knowledge of both male and female reproductive organs and how they work!

Maths: A – (1+1+1+1) Charlotte managed to count all her 'lovers', keeping a tab of her magic number.

French: A – Another subject that Charlotte has excelled in. Her best piece of French was the group project completed with exchange student Patrice.

English: D – Charlotte often fails to understand the real meaning of words, particularly when they come out of the mouth of a certain William McKenzie.

BACKGROUND

Charlotte Hinchcliffe is the most popular girl at Rudge Park Comprehensive. Throughout *The Inbetweeners* series, to the shock of his mates, she takes a liking to

CHARLOTTE 'BIG JUGS' HINCHCLIFFE IS PLAYED BY EMILY ATACK.

Will and the pair have several 'encounters' – some good, some very bad.

We're introduced to Charlotte in Series One, Episode Four: 'Girlfriend'. The lads are at a party and they hear Charlotte may be going. This gets them very excited and, before she even arrives, they are already talking about how fit she is. Jay reckons Charlotte has to get special bras made because, 'not only are her tits so big, but they are perfectly round'.

'They're like porn-star tits!' adds Neil.

Charlotte first meets Will when she catches him trying to drink her champagne at the party. Much to his surprise, they get talking and she decides to take him upstairs. The encounter is short-lived when bully Mark Donovan walks in to catch Will and Charlotte (Donovan's ex) kissing. Will's first chance with Charlotte is very quickly over.

A few days after the party in school, Charlotte lets Will know that she's already had 11 lovers! What she doesn't realise is that Will's still a virgin and she invites him round at the weekend for a bit of you know what.

Her next attempt with Will doesn't go as smoothly as both would have wanted and it becomes obvious, very quickly, that Will is a virgin. After having to stop midway through his awkward motions, she tells him he can't count that as sex and throws him out.

Later that same episode, Charlotte breaks Will's heart

when she takes part in a school 'Blind Date' show, telling the audience she's been messing around with boys and is now after a real man. She continues to pop up in several episodes, including the school fashion show and as a barmaid at an under-eighteens club night (when Simon gets beaten up by a kid!).

FUNNIEST SCENE

When Charlotte invites Will round to her house, she tells him she's already had numerous sexual partners. To save face, Will adds a few notches to his own notch-less bedpost, but in the confusion ends up admitting that when he was thirteen he had sex with an eleven-year-old. This is a great scene between the two as we see Will crack under the pressure, while Charlotte enjoys watching him squirm.

LOVES

Sex
Vibrating love eggs
Attention
French exchange students
Bedrooms at parties

HATES

Virgins
Will's moves in the bedroom
Mark Donovan

HOBBIES

Charlotte's one and only hobby is sex. It's all she talks about... and all anyone talking about her talks about! If she's not at university, Charlotte can usually be found in an upstairs room of a house party.

> *Did you know?*
> Actress Emily Atack who plays Charlotte says that filming the 'sex' scene with Simon Bird (Will) was her funniest moment on set: 'It was all getting a bit awkward in places, where certain parts would touch, that was probably the funniest. I was crying (with laughter) at the time!'

Chloe

Jay's girlfriend for just one episode – the final episode of Series Two – is Chloe. She attends another school away from Rudge Park Comprehensive and was rumoured to have 'got off' with Donovan's psycho mate, David Glover. After Jay's dad Terry tells him to keep tabs on her, she eventually dumps him for being too needy and obsessive. Chloe seems to bring out the sensitive side in Jay, as in this particular episode he tones down his bravado out of respect for his new girlfriend. She is played by actress Lizzie Stables, who after

JAMES BUCKLEY ENJOYS A SPOT OF SHOPPING IN LONDON.

appearing in *The Inbetweeners* featured in the British gangster film *The Big I Am* (2010), about a young, small-time criminal who joins a London gang.

Chris D'Amato

Carli's younger brother appears in the 'Bunk Off' episode, where Simon is sick on his head, and once again in the final episode, when Simon tries to climb through the window into Carli's room but mistakenly lands in Chris's bedroom. He is played by Deo Simcox – a young actor who has made numerous appearances in comedy shows and dramas – and whose acting credits include *Torchwood*, *Casualty* and *Ruddy Hell! It's Harry and Paul*. Deo has also been a voiceover artist for a couple of popular video games: in 2008, he provided a voice for *Fable II* and then, in 2009, he voiced a number of characters in *Dragon Age: Origins*.

d is for...

Daisy

Daisy, who appears in the 'Duke of Edinburgh Awards' episode, used to babysit Will when he was younger. She works at the old people's home and arranges for the lads to volunteer there as part of their Duke of Edinburgh Award. Daisy agrees to go out to dinner with Will as a thank-you for working one of her shifts, but in the end one thing leads to another. However, she has to avoid his advances due to an embarrassing encounter with a wig. The part of Daisy is played by English actress Catherine Steadman, who has appeared in many British TV shows, including *The Bill*, *Holby City* and *Law & Order: UK*. After 2009, she had recurring parts in *Doctors*

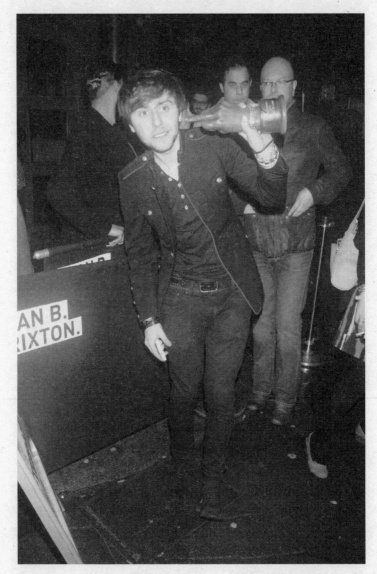

JAMES BUCKLEY AT THE NME AWARDS.

and the period drama *The Tudors*. In 2011, her biggest role came when she landed a part in the sequel to the 2008 film *Outpost* entitled *Outpost: Black Sun*.

Danny Moore

A pupil of Rudge Park Comp, Danny Moore comes from a rough family on the notorious 'Northwood' estate and features in the 'Work Experience' episode. He is first seen in the school corridor, where he hears a comment from Jay and mistakenly thinks it came from Simon, following which the youngster threatens him. Later on in the episode, he sees Simon on the dance floor of an under-eighteens disco and gets him back for the earlier altercation, kicking him repeatedly in the groin. Danny Moore is played by the young London comedian Charlie Wernham; Charlie first appeared on British TV in 2008 when he auditioned as a stand-up for *Britain's Got Talent*. He subsequently made the semi-final of the competition but, more importantly, achieved greater exposure for himself as a comic actor. After *The Inbetweeners*, he went on to appear in an episode of the acclaimed BBC drama *Ashes to Ashes* (2009) and, in the same year, appeared in the E4 sketch show *School of Comedy* as well as the BBC series *Ruddy Hell! It's Harry and Paul*.

David Glover

David is one of Donovan's goons; he hangs around with the school psychopath and mimics his loutish behaviour. He appears in three episodes and is first seen in Episode One of Series One, when Will asks him if he is in the right class, to which he responds in a somewhat aggressive fashion. He can also be seen in Episode One of Series Two on a field trip, when the four guys and new girl Lauren knock on his door at the hostel to ask if they can come to the party. Finally, he makes an appearance in the last episode of Series Two, when it is rumoured that Jay's girlfriend Chloe has also pulled David. It is unclear if this actually happens as Jay convinces Neil not to ask him; however, when Jay confronts Chloe, she is somewhat cagey about the subject but denies knowing David. Richard Hart plays David Glover and, to date, *The Inbetweeners* is his only TV credit.

Dizzee Rascal

Iain Morris and Damon Beesley, writers of *The Inbetweeners*, have been rumoured to be penning a sitcom about the life of UK rapper Dizzee Rascal. In March 2011, a source told the *Sun* newspaper: 'Damon and Iain like the idea of making a funny show about a rapper.' It is also rumoured that Dizzee would play a

IT IS RUMOURED THAT WRITERS IAIN MORRIS AND DAMON BEESLEY'S NEXT PROJECT COULD BE A COMEDY ABOUT THE LIFE OF RAPPER DIZZEE RASCAL.

cameo as he has expressed an interest in getting involved with acting: 'Dizzee is a big personality with loads of charisma and the writers think he would be the ideal subject for the show. It's just a question of whether or not he has the acting ability to pull it off.' Dizzee's acting aspirations were revealed by the *News of the World* when he made it known that he would love to become the first black James Bond after he topped a poll beating off stiff competition from Will Smith, Jay-Z and Barack Obama!

Morris and Beesley have apparently held a series of meetings with the rapper; however, it is still unclear what structure the new sitcom would take, although with Dizzee's eventful life they definitely wouldn't be short of material.

Real name Dylan Mills, Dizzee Rascal was born on 1 October 1985 and grew up in East London, where he was raised by his mother after his father died when he was still a young boy. Growing up, he seemed destined for a life of trouble and disruption after getting expelled from a number of schools and becoming involved in petty crime. However, the one class he did enjoy in school was music and, from this, he joined various theatre workshops to develop his passion. In his mid- to late teens, he became an amateur hip-hop and garage DJ. After developing a talent rapping, Mills stepped in front of the turntables and took the mic under the name 'Dizzee Rascal'. His first album, *Boy in da Corner* (2003), propelled him into the world of UK hip-hop, and his other three albums, *Showtime*, *Maths + English* and *Tongue N' Cheek*, have all received critical acclaim and sold in their thousands.

In his short career, Dizzee Rascal has so far managed to create gold- and platinum-selling albums. He has also received a number of awards and nominations, including the Mercury Prize (2003); he has his own record label named 'Dirtee Stank' and has even appeared on BBC's *Newsnight* with Jeremy Paxman. There are sure to be many incredible moments in Dizzee's life that could be exploited by Morris and Beesley, if a sitcom was to appear on our screens.

DRINKING GAMES

When they decide to bunk off school for the day, the first thing on the minds of the Inbetweeners is getting hold of some booze. When Will actually manages to get served, Jay decides a drinking game is in order. With a bottle of gin and some party snacks, the foursome pour shots and down them at Jay's command. He even makes Simon a cocktail of vodka, whisky and crème de menthe.

Fans of the show have devised their own drinking game based on its characters, sayings and scenes. In fact, it's become so popular that a Facebook page, 'The

Official Inbetweeners Drinking Game', has over 20,000 people who 'like' it! The rules are as follows:

RULE ONE: EVERY TIME JAY UTTERS THE WORDS 'CLUNGE', 'GASH', 'SPUNK', 'BELL-END' OR THE PHRASE 'UP TO THE BALLS', DOWN A SHOT.

RULE TWO: EVERY TIME JAY UTTERS A PHRASE FOR THE FEMALE ANATOMY OR HIS OWN GENITALIA THAT YOU HAVE NEVER HEARD USED BEFORE, DOWN ANOTHER SHOT.

RULE THREE: EACH TIME SOMEONE REFERS TO NEIL'S DAD AS BEING GAY AND NEIL SAYS, 'OI, MY DAD'S NOT BENT!', DOWN A CAN.

RULE FOUR: CRACK INTO THE VODKA WHENEVER THERE'S ANY GAG ABOUT BODILY FLUIDS.

RULE FIVE: DRINK A DOUBLE WHEN THE PHRASES 'HUMPING' OR 'PORKING' ARE USED TO REFER TO SEXUAL INTERCOURSE.

RULE SIX: CONSUME A CAN OF CHEAP CIDER EVERY TIME THE BOYS ATTEMPT TO GET SERVED ALCOHOL, 'PULL SOME BIRDS' OR END UP ANNOYING SIXTH-FORM HEAD MR GILBERT.

RULE SEVEN: IF WILL ENDS UP TIED UP, BULLIED OR GAGGED AND BOUND IN AN UNUSUAL MANNER, HAVE A CAN.

RULE EIGHT: DRINK WHENEVER SIMON OR ANY OTHER MEMBER OF THE CAST SAYS THE WORD 'BRILLIANT' AFTER ANOTHER PERSON HAS MADE A JOKE ABOUT THEM.

RULE NINE: AT ANY POINT IF SIMON TRIES TO TALK TO CARLI AND LOOKS LIKE A CREEPY TIT, DRINK A CAN OF ANYTHING.

RULE TEN: IF THERE'S ANY REFERENCE TO SIMON, JAY OR NEIL WANTING TO HAVE SEX WITH WILL'S MUM, DRINK A SHOT OF ANYTHING.

RULE ELEVEN: WHENEVER MR GILBERT REFERS TO THE CHARACTERS BY THEIR LAST NAMES, DOWN A CAN AND A SHOT.

Did you know?
There's also a Facebook page dedicated to a fourth series of the show. With almost 70,000 people 'liking' the page and an online petition, it's a great accolade to the fans' love for the sitcom.

Driving Examiner

At the start of the 'Thorpe Park' episode, Simon passes his test with the help of an extremely lenient, but horny driving instructor. He fails at the first hurdle when asked if he can out read a number plate; however, she forgives him as he has nice eyes. The driving examiner is played by Oriane Messina, who has written some of Britain's most successful comedies including *The Impressions Show*, *Comedy Lab* and *Green Wing*; as an actress, she has also starred in the likes of *Miranda*, *Not Going Out* and *Ruddy Hell! It's Harry and Paul*.

e is for...

E4

Launched in 2001, E4 has been home to a raft of top British shows including *The Inbetweeners*, *Misfits and Shameless*, as well as hit US sitcoms including *Ugly Betty*, *Scrubs* and *Friends* (until autumn 2011).

The channel's most successful broadcast to date was on 11 October 2010, when more than 3.7 million viewers tuned into an episode of *The Inbetweeners*. In fact, the show makes up six of the Top 10 Most Viewed Broadcasts on the channel!

The Inbetweeners was the first sitcom commissioned directly for the channel. Simon Bird (Will) told *Digital Spy* that, when the show first started, E4's backing was a big help: 'A lot of us were doing TV for the first time. There's a bit of pressure on it, being as it's the first [sitcom] they've ever done but E4's pretty popular now so it should do well.'

Connections between *The Inbetweeners* and the channel also include writer Damon Beesley. Before

THE BOYS ARE FANS OF THEIR HOME CHANNEL, E4.

setting up Bwark Productions (makers of the show), he enjoyed a stint at E4 as commissioning editor for comedy and entertainment. In this role, he was responsible for such award-winning shows as *Banzai* and *Big Brother's Little Brother*.

The channel's connection with comedy also runs deep. Since 2006, it has sponsored the E4 UdderBELLY venue at the Edinburgh Fringe and Brighton Festivals. E4 has also showcased the TV appearance of Jessica Knappett (Lisa from *The Inbetweeners'* movie) in *Meet The Parents*.

The Inbetweeners have also revealed that they're fans of the channel. In an E4 web chat, Blake (Neil) told fans he likes *Misfits* and *Scrubs*. Simon (Will) is also a fan of *Misfits*, while James (Jay) agrees with Blake regarding *Scrubs* and Joe (Simon) kicks it old school with *Friends*.

> *Did you know?*
> The connection with Channel 4 didn't end with the third series. *The Inbetweeners'* movie was funded by sister channel Film4.

Emily Atack

You may know Emily Atack better for her role as Charlotte 'Big Jugs' Hinchcliffe. Born in Bedfordshire, on 18 December 1989, Emily is the oldest of three.

Thanks to her parents, she was destined for a life in showbiz: her mum Kate Robbins is also an actress, while her dad Keith Atack is a musician.

Although best known for her role in *The Inbetweeners*, Emily has made several other TV appearances. These include presenting the 2011 BBC3 programme *Ready, Steady, Drink*, where she highlighted the dangers of alcohol as part of the channel's 'Dangerous Pleasures' season. Emily revealed to the *Mirror* that, as part of the programme, she joined a gang of students on a night out, where she drank 15 shots of vodka: 'It was an experiment and I had to keep up with the students. I've had some hangovers before but that was something else. I just wanted to die! I went back to see the students and they had lectures, but they seemed all right. They must have built up a tolerance to it. I had to stop filming so I could be sick. I must have done it about five times.'

She was also a contestant on the hit ITV show *Dancing On Ice* (2010), reaching the eighth week with professional ice skater Fred Palascak, after being told by judge Jason Gardiner that she was 'lazy'. Her other TV appearances include *Heartbeat*, *Victoria Wood's Midlife Christmas* and *Rock & Chips*.

ACTRESS EMILY ATACK (CHARLOTTE) IS FROM A SHOWBUSINESS BACKGROUND. HER MOTHER IS AN ACTRESS AND HER FATHER IS A MUSICIAN.

Did you know?
After exiting *Dancing On Ice*, Emily told *Digital Spy* that she thinks Simon Bird (Will) should take to the ice, although she admitted that Blake Harrison (Neil) would have a better chance, thanks to the body-popping skills he's always showing off. Blake visited the set to see Emily performing on *Dancing On Ice* and the lads all supported her by voting every day.

Emily Head

Carli D'Amato's character in the hit series is played by Londoner Emily Head: born on 15 December 1988, after training at one of the city's dance schools, she attended the famous BRIT School in Croydon. The BRIT School is an establishment for theatre and performing arts which has boasted some famous alumni over the past few years, including Dane Bowers, Lynden David Hall and The Feeling to name but a few. She also attended the school with her *Inbetweeners'* co-star Blake Harrison.

Before taking to our TV screens, Emily took part in many theatre productions while at dance school and

(LEFT TO RIGHT): EMILY HEAD, BELINDA STEWART-WILSON AND HANNAH TOINTON.

then later at The BRIT School. Her other TV work includes the ITV drama *Trial and Retribution*, *Doc Martin* (starring Martin Clunes) and the BBC daytime drama *Doctors*. In late 2010, she took part in a BBC Radio 2 comedy showcase also featuring Ricky Tomlinson, Clive Anderson and Andy Parsons.

After starring in three successful series of *The Inbetweeners*, Emily revealed to the *Mirror* newspaper that she was very sad that the show had finished and wished there could be a fourth series. She was, however, excited about the prospect of a film on the horizon.

In 2011, before filming *The Inbetweeners'* movie, Emily revealed that even she did not know what was contained in the infamous text message sent from Carli to Simon at the end of the final episode of Series Three – presumably to protect the development of their relationship in the 2011 film.

Emily and Blake Harrison (who plays Neil in the show) have remained friends since filming the series and tweeted each other during the filming. As Blake had started work in Malia, Emily was waiting to join them: 'What's the weather like out there? I'm in danger of packing everything I own.'

Emily comes from a highly theatrical family: her younger sister Daisy has also appeared in a number of British TV shows, including *Trial & Retribution*, *Doc Martin*, *Holby City* and *Doctors*. The girls' father is

EMILY HEAD COMES FROM A THEATRICAL FAMILY — HER FATHER IS ANTHONY HEAD AND HER SISTER DAISY IS ALSO AN ACTRESS.

Anthony Head, an English actor and musician who sprang to fame in the Nescafe Gold Blend adverts in the late 1980s, when he appeared in 12 commercials. In 1996, the biggest break in his career came with the part of Rupert Giles in the American teen drama *Buffy the Vampire Slayer* starring alongside Sarah Michelle Gellar. The highly successful show ran for seven seasons through to 2003. After living in the USA during his time on *Buffy*, he moved home to continue his acting career in established TV shows such as *Spooks*, *Silent Witness* and *Monarch of the Glen*. In 2003, he took the role of prime minister in the hugely successful series *Little Britain* starring comedians Matt Lucas and David Walliams.

The year 2011 saw Anthony star alongside Meryl Streep in the hotly anticipated film *The Iron Lady*, the story of Margaret Thatcher's reign as prime minister during the 1980s. He plays the part of Geoffrey Howe, Thatcher's longest-serving cabinet minister.

'Exam Time': Series Two, Episode Six

It's the end of term at Rudge Park Comp and the boys should be preparing for their AS Levels. Will is feeling the pressure and has decided to shut all his mates out until the exams are over. Simon, on the other hand, is more preoccupied with impressing Carli D'Amato, so, when she asks if she can go around to his house to revise, he's all for it!

It's not only Simon who is getting distracted by girls, though. Jay has met a real-life girl called Chloe and, although she won't join in his filthy thoughts, he's extremely happy that he's actually found someone. The final Inbetweener Neil is not suffering from any of the distractions of the others: he's not stressing out (like Will), he's not chasing girls (like Simon) and he's not in a relationship (like Jay). Neil's just being Neil, and paying far too little attention to his studies.

Will, however, seems much more prepared. With a revision timetable that took two days to make and enough energy drinks to keep a team of marathon runners going for a week, everything seems to be on schedule. The only problem is that Will isn't actually revising: putting all this effort into planning his schedule, creating charts, preparing his workspace and trying to focus has left him starting to panic about actually learning stuff for the exams!

Will's not the only one with things on his mind: when Carli goes over to Simon's, she reveals that she's split with boyfriend Tom, sending Simon into romance overload. To set the mood, he immediately gets the music on, tries to get Carli off the subject of revision and suggests watching a movie. Unfortunately for Si,

Carli is more conscientious than he is and, even worse, she manages to convince him to help her with revision for geography, even though he doesn't study it himself!

Will's revision timetable isn't quite going to plan either. Despite his über-organisation, he's on the verge of a breakdown as he tells Simon, while cramming in the school library: 'Nothing's fucking going in!'

Simon warns Will about drinking so many energy drinks, telling him from his experience they can give you a serious case of diarrhoea.

After Neil tells Jay he thinks Chloe went out with David Glover from their year a while back, Jay starts to get jealous. He seeks advice from his dad but, as always, he isn't much help: 'Women are like fairground rides, fucking mental! Check where she is all the time, that's the only way you'll be totally sure she's not sucking off this other bloke.'

Although Chloe tells Jay she's never heard of this other guy, he follows his dad's advice and starts following her every move to guarantee she's not cheating.

Simon's luck seems to be going much more smoothly than Jay's as his plan with Carli has actually worked. While the two of them are in his bedroom having a study session, they end up kissing when Carli thanks Si for all his help.

Will, on the other hand, is having completely different problems. On the morning of his last exam he's starting to feel the effects of the intensive revision schedule. After staying up all night to cram and drinking copious amounts of energy drink, both head and bowels are starting to suffer. Still, he makes it to the exam unwashed and absolutely wired on caffeine. Shortly into the exam, Will's bowels launch into action as Simon had warned and, when Mr Gilbert refuses him the fourth toilet break in an hour, unearthly sounds start to resonate from inside him. This ends with him shitting himself and he is left waddling to the bathroom!

Later that night, at The Fox and Hounds, Jay, Neil and Simon have actually managed to get served. Jay's planning on meeting up with Chloe, while Simon and Neil are left wondering where Will is. It's then that Will walks into the pub wearing his school blazer and some lost-property tracksuit bottoms, carrying a bag containing his soiled trousers and underpants. Much to his disbelief, he actually manages to get served and so he starts to drown his sorrows in numerous pints of lager.

While Will's still at the bar, Chloe meets up with the guys. Jay is eager to introduce her to the gang but she takes him outside for a 'chat'. This ends in her breaking things off following his stalker-like behaviour – 'I think you're a bit too sensitive for me' – and it's one of the few times where Jay shows any emotion.

THE BOYS WITH THEIR BRITISH ACADEMY OF TELEVISION AUDIENCE AWARD. IT'S THE ONLY AWARD VOTED FOR BY THE PUBLIC SO IT JUST GOES TO SHOW HOW MANY FANS THE SHOW HAS.

Things aren't going too well for Simon either because Carli comes to the pub with her supposedly ex-boyfriend Tom. What's worse is that, before Simon finds out they're back on, he hands Carli a CD he's made for her and admits to always having feelings for her.

The episode ends with a teary Jay breaking his news to the others, Simon admitting he was dumped by Carli and Will realising that he has a new school year to look forward to... where he can expect loads of insults related to his exam incident!

Did you know?
If you look closely at the CD Simon makes Carli in this episode, you can read the titles of several famous love songs, including 'Lady in Red' by Chris De Burgh and Bryan Adams' 'Everything I Do'. But if you look really closely you can also see that track nine on the list is 'My Hairy Mole' by Boyzone! Obviously not a real track in the repertoire of the famous Irish band, but a sneaky comedy extra added into the show.

f is for...

Facebook and Twitter

Not only is *The Inbetweeners* a big success onscreen, but thanks to the support of its fans the show has made a huge impact online.

With over 2.5 million 'likes', *The Inbetweeners'* Facebook page is certainly one of the best for admirers of the show to get involved with. Packed with lots of love from fans, favourite quotes, rumours, discussions and photos, it's a must for any *Inbetweeners'* enthusiast on Facebook. And there are plenty of other pages dedicated to the comedy foursome with thousands more followers, showing just what a big hit it has been.

In the league of E4 hits, the show ranks well in terms

of Facebook followers. *Skins* tops the list with an impressive 2.8 million 'likes' followed by *The Inbetweeners* and then *Misfits*, with over 1 million. Other E4 shows with *Inbetweeners'* connections include *PhoneShop* (featuring Martin Trenaman – Simon Cooper's dad) with over 28,000 fans and Simon Bird's sitcom *Friday Night Dinner* has several thousand, too.

Fans can catch up with others on Facebook and share their favourite moments of *The Inbetweeners* but if they're more interested in the people involved in making the show, then Twitter is the place to be.

Several of the show's cast and crew have made a big hit on Twitter. Top of the list is Blake Harrison (Neil), who is a regular tweeter with over 28,000 followers. Blake's Twitter profile describes him as 'an actor, millwall fan, cardigan wearer, comic book reader and have a soft spot for gingers'. His tweets reveal insights and plenty of info about filming, chilling out with friends – and his love for his girlfriend and Nandos!

Next on the list of Twitter followers is Emily Atack (Charlotte Hinchcliffe), with almost 10,000 people following her tweets. Emily's profile includes a nod to her role as Charlotte and her stint on the celebrity reality show *Dancing On Ice*.

Co-writer Iain Morris also has around 10,000 followers. He describes himself as 'Inbetweeners, some conchords, former sidekick, peep show hanger-on, all low quality work considered'. Morris follows a collection of comedy tweeters, including Jimmy Carr, David Baddiel, Dave Gorman, Simon Pegg and 'Godfather of Twitter' Stephen Fry. His tweets include mentions of Neil, Simon, Will and Joe – including loads of comments about making the movie.

Emily Head (Carli D'Amato) and Henry Lloyd-Hughes (Mark Donovan) can also be found on the social network. Although they don't have quite so many followers as some of the others, there's still a lot of love for the pair, with around 1,000 followers each.

Best Tweets

Here's a few of the finest tweets by some of *The Inbetweeners'* cast and crew:

Blakeharrison23 (Blake Harrison): 'finally have wi-fi in my room! Looking forward to Skyeping a very special ginge!.....& after I speak to Paul Scholes I may talk to my gf.'

Iainkevanmorris (Iain Morris): 'It's got spunk stains and blowjob sticker. But seriously, it does smell of buckley's farts.'

EmAtack (Emily Atack): 'I physically cannot watch "deal or no deal"...It breaks my soul. And i curse myself for slightly fancying Noel Edmonds.'

Emily_head (Emily Head): 'Just got back to my flat and there is a bright yellow fiat cinquecento parked outside...seriously...'

Matineeidle (Henry Lloyd-Hughes): 'I ran for the bus, so I'm sweatin a bit, other passengers giving me a bit of a wide birth...'

To find out more about any of the *Inbetweeners* mentioned, just search their profile names on Twitter.com.

Fans

It seems the fans of *The Inbetweeners* are some of the most dedicated around. Simon Bird (Will) admitted to *Buzz* that, 'People shout a lot of insults at me because they're quotes from *The Inbetweeners*. I get called "Briefcase Wanker", "Bus Wanker" and sometimes just plain "Wanker!"' But he says he doesn't take these insults to heart, explaining, 'It's always done in such a nice way that I don't mind – I like to think it's all affectionate abuse.'

THE INBETWEENERS IS A BIG HIT WITH TEENAGERS.

Simon told *ShortList* about the weirdest request he's ever had from a fan: 'The most unexpected one was a guy who asked me to sign his penis. I drew the line there. Not literally.' And he's not the only Inbetweener who's had to deal with this type of thing. In an E4 web chat with the guys, Joe Thomas (Simon) also revealed he's had the 'pleasure' of meeting a fan's intimate places. Asked what's the funniest thing an *Inbetweeners'* fan has ever done, Joe said, 'A bloke got his cock out', with James (Jay) questioning: 'How do you know he was a fan?'

There seem to be perks with having such a big fan base, however. In the same web chat, one fan asked the guys if they would ever date a fan. James answered yes, with Blake confirming, 'He's not joking!'

During filming for *The Inbetweeners'* movie, Simon admits that attention from the fans was a lot to deal with and that the cast and crew were 'overrun'. He went on to say, 'There were more people than we could deal with – it was carnage!'

The attention wasn't enough to put the movie-makers off giving the fans their chance to be involved, though. Fans aged between 18 and 35 could apply to be an extra on the E4 website. There were several options that they could apply for, including filming at an event at the famous Faces nightclub in Essex for a club scene or travelling to Spain as a single or as a group to take part.

During the 'Rude Road Trip' for Comic Relief in January 2011, the boys described support from their fans as 'really nice', after a group of them had waited at 'Titty Ho' in Northamptonshire for hours just to catch a glimpse of the comedy foursome.

The support spread to Twitter, too, where fans suggested loads of smutty place names for the gang to find on their trip. In fact, #rudetrip became a top trend, with some of the best fan suggestions including Cockermouth, Twatt and Fingringhoe!

'Fashion Show': Series Three, Episode One

At the start of Series Three, it's back to school for the Inbetweeners. It's been a busy summer for the lads, especially Jay, who's passed his driving test and got his 'gay' ear pierced. When questioned on the 'new look',

FANS WERE EAGER TO CATCH A GLIMPSE OF THE CAST WHEN THEY WERE FILMING THE RUDE ROAD TRIP FOR COMIC RELIEF.

he reveals that he wants to keep his look fresh for the school charity fashion show the following day.

Will takes this opportunity to get on his soapbox, telling the others he's against the whole idea of good-looking people judging other good-looking people. Jay disagrees with this theory, thinking only of the benefits for him: 'I don't give a shit what you think about it, because when I'm up there modelling I'll have the pick of the snatch!' What Jay doesn't realise is that all the models have already been asked, including Simon, thanks to organiser Carli.

At school, head of sixth form Mr Gilbert reveals that pupil Alistair Scott is returning to the school after recovering from kidney failure. The fashion show will donate everything raised towards a new dialysis machine for the local hospital, but, despite the good cause and Alistair's trauma, Jay refuses to take part in his welcome: 'I never liked him when he was well, I never liked him when he was ill and I don't like him now he's getting better. Simples.'

Despite Will's 'moral objection' to the fashion show, Gilbert decides he must be in charge of collecting the money for the event. Neil is keener to assist and tells Carli he'll help get the models dressed through the show so he can see 'some close-up flange for charity'. Despite Jay's eagerness to get involved as a model, he's still turned down.

the inbetweeners A-Z

On the night of the show, Will is still making his feelings heard, while Neil has his own disappointments in the form of a curtain up between the boys' dressing area and the girls; also the only other person who offered to be a dresser is Mr 'Paedo' Kennedy. His night starts to look up, however, as Charlotte Hinchcliffe turns up as a special guest.

Despite all the problems, the fashion show starts off well and, when Will's asked to fill in by Charlotte, his morals go out the window and, next thing you know, he's in a pair of skinny jeans and denim waistcoat faster than you can say Charlotte 'Big Jugs' Hinchcliffe. To his great disappointment, however, even after his involve-ment in the show, Charlotte still insists he has no chance.

Meanwhile, backstage Simon is also being asked to fill in. Thanks to another model's hairy back, Carli asks Si if he'll walk the 'sexy finale' with her, wearing just a pair of Speedos and a hat. Jay and Neil point out that the outfit won't leave much to the imagination and that walking down the runway with the sexy Carli could lead to a boner in front of the whole school!

Thanks to stern concentration, Simon manages to keep his male urges at bay but what he doesn't realise is that one of his balls is hanging out the Speedos for the whole show! Everyone in the room, including his dad and Mr Gilbert, is aware of this fashion faux pas. It's not until he's backstage that he finds out what's happened, whereupon an angry Carli storms off, accusing him of ruining her big night.

The night ends with the lads on their own again, Jay with an ear infection and Simon with even less chance with Carli than he had before. Just another typical day then!

Did you know?
James Buckley (Jay) has both of his ears pierced. He also has several tattoos, including a star on his chest.

FHM

Male fans of *The Inbetweeners* will no doubt know that three of the stars from the show appeared as cover girls in September 2010's edition of *FHM* in conjunction with the start of the third series. Emily Atack, Emily

Head and Hannah Tointon all featured in the lads' magazine, scantily clad in sexy work clothes. The raunchy photos featured the girls pictured as a threesome and separately modelling around old-school telephones, desks and photocopiers, all three taking full advantage of the 'sexy secretary' tags. The shoot was centred around the theme of the girls graduating from high school and entering into the real world, presumably to work in office buildings!

In the same edition of the magazine, the boys from *The Inbetweeners* feature on the back cover modelling stylish clothes from the *FHM* collection, again to illustrate them growing up as they enter their final year in school. During the shoot, when *FHM* asked about their own fashion styles, James Buckley revealed that he used to think he was cool but now he realises he dresses like an old man and that, when he was younger, he would wear his mother's sequinned scarf! Even more alarmingly, the girls revealed that Blake Harrison was very upset that he didn't get to wear stockings and suspenders, too.

Belinda Stewart-Wilson, who plays Polly McKenzie (Will's mum), has also appeared in *FHM* in January 2011, pictured in glamorous underwear to the theme of the sexy older woman. During the shoot, she comments on the boys' characters in the show and how they are fascinated with her and older women in general. She admitted to *FHM* that she was often embarrassed about things in the show: 'She's become incredibly popular by doing very little. I went to the read-through for the third series and I was literally blushing all the way through from what they were saying about me. It's filthy, but that's why it's popular.'

Belinda and the three other girls featured in *FHM* have all been nominated in the poll to find the '100 Sexiest Girls of 2011'.

'Field Trip': Series Two, Episode One

Series Two starts off with a bang as the four Inbetweeners visit the seaside town of Swanage on a geography and sociology field trip (despite the fact that Neil doesn't do geography or sociology!).

Will, being his usual sensible self, suggests the four use the field trip to try something different like a leisurely boat ride; he has even taken the trouble to ring ahead at the harbour and check if they can book a vessel! But the other three have different plans in mind, with Simon wanting to get drunk and pull girls, while Jay and Neil are on the hunt for the mythical Swanage MILF.

After being moved from the back of the bus by bully Mark Donovan & co, Jay ends up sitting next to

GORGEOUS HANNAH TOINTON, WHO PLAYS TARA, OUT ON THE TOWN WITH FELLOW ACTRESSES CHARLEY WEBB, ROXANNE MCKEE AND JENNA-LOUISE COLEMAN.

Mr Gilbert, while Will manages to land a seat next to new girl Lauren Harris. This takes the sour edge off the field trip for Will, 'who is more used to field trips to places like the Alps or Barcelona, than shitty English seaside towns'.

Jay's main priority is to find a fabled seaside MILF, who apparently, according to one of his bullshit stories, chooses one schoolboy each year for a special lesson! All he needs to do in Swanage to find this real woman is ask the right MILF if she will lick his Cornetto…

On arrival, Lauren asks Will if she can sit with him at lunch so naturally he starts to think things are looking up on the female front but Simon throws a spanner into the works and admits he thinks she's pretty fit, too, pissing off Will. In a Will-esque attempt to impress Lauren, he decides to go for his Yoda impression but, rather than this getting him one step closer, she thinks he may have Asperger's and decides to work with Simon on the trip, leaving Will with Big John instead.

Meanwhile, Jay and Neil continue to search for the seaside MILF and, as part of the 'surveys' needed for the field trip, Jay approaches the women of Swanage. He asks one of them:

1. How did you get into town today?
2. How often do you use public transport?
3. And do you wear stockings and that?

While we don't get to hear the fourth and final question, it ends with a roundhouse slap to Jay's face. We can only guess he asked her to lick his Cornetto!

Back at the hostel, Will finds out Lauren thinks Simon is quite the hottie and his jealousy gets even worse as he warns Simon off.

As part of Neil's arrangement to come on the trip as Paedo Kennedy's helper, he agrees to go swimming in the sea in a pair of Speedos provided by his teacher. In return for this obvious act of paedo-age, Kennedy gives Neil a bottle of vodka and tells him not to mention any of this to Mr Gilbert, head of sixth (wonder why?).

Despite knowing the vodka was obtained by pimping Neil out to Kennedy, the other Inbetweeners are pleased and, along with Lauren, head down the hall to a party. There's no surprise when the five are turned away by Donovan, who also takes Neil's reward.

Jay and Neil return to the search for yummy mummies and Simon decides this is a better chance than ever to make a move on Lauren. Still adamant Simon and Lauren won't hook up, Will escorts them both to Lauren's room, hanging around like a third wheel as the pair cuddle and express their affection for each other.

Later that night, as the four are tucked up in bed, Paedo Kennedy makes another appearance, popping into the room to give Neil a leg massage to assist with lactic acid flow after the tiring swim. Thanks to Mr Gilbert's intervention and Neil's complete inability to be aware of anything happening in his surroundings, the incident is brushed under the carpet.

The following day, Neil and Simon bump into Si's long-term love interest, Carli, who is also on the trip. Will takes his chance to get Si out of the picture and convinces him to blow off his planned date with Lauren and spend the time with Carli instead. Like a snivelling little worm, Will runs off to Lauren and tells her that Simon has blown her off, in the process convincing her to go on a boat trip he has arranged later that day.

While Simon and Will battle it out, Jay and Neil continue their hunt for older women. With little time left, Jay convinces himself he's found her: a grey-haired, wrinkle-faced, 60+ woman, running an ice-cream kiosk on the pier. Hardly the yummy mummy he'd promised, but he puts a positive spin on her appearance: 'She's probably just got an old face, must be all the jizz she's had on it!'

So, in his last attempt for some Swanage vage, he orders his Cornetto and asks the woman if she wants to lick it. Unsurprisingly, she's not the nympho he was after and, having tried to explain that he wants her to suck him off, he legs it with Neil and Si. The three meet up with 'Captain Cockwash' (Will) at the harbour, who's preparing the boat for his date with Lauren.

Against Will's protests, they decide to take the boat out, with Jay giving the passing public his trademark 'Wanker' sign.

In his next bright move of the day, Jay rocks Simon off the boat, landing him in the freezing cold water. As he clambers back on, speaking in tongues and slurring his words, Will panics that he'll go into hypothermia and gets Neil to strip off Simon's wet clothes, delicately placing a sock on his extremely cold cock. As they attempt to get back to the harbour, they find out the engine has been broken with fishing line Neil threw aboard. This leaves the four on a boat with no power, a dead fish and a nude teenager. In a panic, Jay releases a flare to call the Sea Police. At the best possible time, Lauren arrives and a crowd gathers. The four eventually get back to land, thanks to a tow from the Sea Police and the field trip to Swanage ends, slightly off-plan.

'First Day': Series One, Episode One

The 'First Day' episode is where the story of *The Inbetweeners* begins. It starts with a very nervous Will McKenzie walking into Rudge Park Comprehensive for the first time. He explains how the divorce of his parents has forced him out of his plush private school and into a state comp. It's good to see that Will hasn't

WILL MACKENZIE (PLAYED BY SIMON BIRD) IS THE NARRATOR OF THE SHOW. HIS FIRST DAY AT THE SCHOOL IS WHERE THE STORY OF OUR FAVOURITE SIXTH-FORMERS BEGINS …

left the etiquette behind altogether as one of a handful of pupils at his new school to be sporting a blazer – and the only one with a briefcase!

But Will doesn't get off to the best start at his new school with either the teachers or the pupils. He starts his day at a welcome meeting in the headmaster's office with Mr Gilbert, head of sixth, and the other new starters. Immediately, he gets on the wrong side of Gilbert – suggesting that maybe the massive green badges all new pupils have to wear may make them targets; the new pupils aren't much better and even 'Briefcase Wanker' Will doesn't want to be seen with 'the freaks'.

Things don't get much better for Will at his first lesson. After locating the class, he strides in and introduces himself to the first kid he finds, opting for the classic handshake approach – not the sort of thing the kids at Rudge Park are accustomed to. This doesn't go down well and Will is turned away cold. To try to make amends, he thinks the best thing to do is to rip into Mr Gilbert: 'Ooo, I'm Mr Gilbert and I just love to suck the headmaster's balls!'

What Will doesn't find out until he's finished his tirade is that Gilbert is standing right behind him. Gilbert takes it on the chin and assigns Inbetweener Simon Cooper to be the new boy's chaperone as they share some of the same classes. This is Will's chance to latch on to someone reasonably normal (or so he thinks).

To calm his nerves, Will decides a good shit is in order. During what he describes as 'one of the more eventful shits of his life', we're introduced to Jay Cartwright and Neil Sutherland, the final two Inbetweeners, as well as school bully Mark Donovan.

With Will poised on the porcelain throne, Simon, Jay and Neil enter the lads' toilets as Jay hands out some expert sex tips he's picked up over the summer break: 'Try to get really deep. Right up to the balls ...' And to Simon: 'While you've spent the summer stalking Carli, I've been out porkin' loads of vage!'

This is the first tip of the series from sexpert Jay Cartwright and certainly not the last. Another first during Will's school-time dump is his meeting with Mark Donovan, who decides to pop his head over Will's cubicle for a quick hello, courtesy of a camera phone. It's not long before Will's mid-poo mug is posted all over the school with the words: 'Hello, I'm Will and I'm doing a shit!' Not the start he'd hoped for!

Eventful shit over, Will heads to the common room to sit with the freaks, where Neil, Jay and Simon are going over their plans for that night: the Rudge Park traditional drink down the Black Horse for all new sixth-formers. Simon's not too keen (worried he won't get served), but, when his fellow pupil and 'family friend' Carli D'Amato (who Jay reckons Simon's been wanking over three times a day, all summer) asks if he'll be going, Simon perks up – quite literally. Jay and Neil spot the sudden movement in Simon's nether regions and follow with a tirade of 'boner' shouts, getting the whole common room to join in.

While Simon's still startled by the 'boner' attention, Will takes his chance to pounce and, leaving the freaks in the dust from his briefcase, offers to save Simon a seat at class. Following his theory that 'anyone can be your friend, you just need to hang around them long enough', at the end of the day Will latches on to Simon, Neil and Jay again, inviting himself to the drink. The others don't seem keen until they see Will's extremely fit mum, who's arrived to pick him up.

After the four Inbetweeners each persuade their parents to loan them some cash, they meet up to embark on a night of heavy drinking and women. Well, that's what they hoped for!

The evening gets off to a bad start because the very first mistake that the group makes is turning up at the wrong venue. While the other sixth-formers are all at the Black Horse, Simon, Will, Neil and Jay arrive at the Black Bull – a dingy and really quite traditional alehouse. Thinking they're at the right place and they must be the first people there because they're 'hardcore', Jay offers to get a round of drinks. It's the second mistake of the night.

Despite managing to secure a drink for himself with

his fake Australian ID, Jay fails to get a pint in for the others, with the barman needing proof of age from each of them. Will then steps in, taking a different, equally ineffective approach. He first attempts to persuade the barman with a sob story of how he's been forced to join a state school, with his mum left broke following her divorce. Unsurprisingly, the tale fails to pull on the barman's heartstrings, leaving Will with one option: brandishing a 'Teenagers Know Your Rights' booklet. He protests that, as he is over 16, he has the right to drink cider, perry or mead in a pub, if eating. This leaves Will, Neil and Simon with a pint of cider each and a ticket for the carvery, having bribed a stranger at the bar with free drinks. Probably not how the four expected the night to start off.

After finally realising they're not even at the right pub, the Inbetweeners eventually get to the Black Horse. Simon sees this as his best chance yet to get close to long-term love interest Carli, but his hopes quickly fly out of the window as she introduces him to her new boyfriend Tom (who drives, much to Simon's annoyance).

The night gets even worse as for the second time Will is refused drinks at the bar, due to no ID. But, instead of accepting defeat and retreating with some dignity intact, Will snaps and points out to the barman that, not only is he not the only underage drinker, he's one of the oldest!

This hilarious rant includes some of Will's best quotes – 'Look at that bum fluff!', 'That bra's got padding in it', 'He looks a bit older because he's uglier…'

Thanks to Will, the barman decides to kick everyone out and, to rub salt into the wounds, Mr Gilbert walks in just as the rant finishes. He is in Gilbert's bad books and, worse still, on Mark Donovan's 'to stab list'. It's the final mistake of the group's first night at The Black Horse (and Bull!) and the perfect end to Will's first day.

First Impressions

Simon Bird (Will) has revealed that, before *The Inbetweeners* first hit our screens, he was worried about what the viewers would think. He told the *Observer* that the cast and crew's lack of TV experience made it hard for them to judge how the show would be first perceived.

'I remember the overriding emotion at the end of filming Series One was relief not to have been fired,' he admitted. Thankfully for everyone, the show immediately started to rake in the viewers.

The first series averaged 459,000 viewers, with 474,000 viewers watching the series finale. Following a number of awards and a lot of media buzz around the show and the cast, the second series was an even bigger hit. It averaged 958,000 viewers, with another 234,000

Simon Bird accepts the BAFTA Television Academy Audience Award from Joanna Page.

viewers watching at 11pm on the time-shift channel E4+1, meaning it was watched by 1.2 million, the highest audience of 2009 for E4! The third series did even better, with the first episode achieving a staggering 2.6m viewers, breaking the record for the highest-ever viewing figure on the channel.

It wasn't just the media and public who loved the show, though. Critics also gave it a great reception with Joe McNally writing in the *Independent* that the show features an 'exquisitely accurate dialogue, capturing the feel of adolescence perfectly', while Will Dean commented in the *Guardian* that it 'captures the pathetic sixth-form male experience quite splendidly'.

Flight of the Conchords

Written by Jemaine Clement and Bret McKenzie, *Flight of the Conchords* is a New Zealand-based comedy about two men trying to make it in New York. The writers of *The Inbetweeners*, Iain Morris and Damon Beesley, co-wrote two episodes: 'The Actor' in Series One (2007) and 'Unnatural Love' from Series Two (2009).

The show follows two main characters, Jemaine and Bret, who set up a band named The Flight of the Conchords to make it big in New York; they are managed by fellow compatriot Murray Hewitt, who is overly protective of the band and their prospects.

The band has attracted a worldwide cult following since they hit the screens in New Zealand in 2000. After making a name for themselves in their home country, the pair then moved on to perform at the Edinburgh Festival in 2002 and 2003, where they received huge admiration from comedy performers and fans alike. In 2004, the band took their music show into a radio adaptation on BBC Radio 2 with well-known British comedians Rob Brydon and Jimmy Carr alongside them; the radio show revolved around the duo trying to make it as a band in London rather than the New York setting for the TV series.

In 2007, broadcaster HBO aired the first episode. After a successful 12 episodes in the first series of *Flight of the Conchords*, a second, 10-episode, series was commissioned in 2009. In this two-year period, the band made numerous TV appearances on talk shows such as the *Late Show with David Letterman* and *Late Night with Conan O'Brien*. Throughout their career, The Flight of the Conchords have continued to take their humorous music show on tour to theatres around the world.

In 2010, one of the greatest honours for any performer was bestowed upon the double act as they were asked to guest-star in an episode of *The Simpsons*. 'Elementary School Musical' featured Jemaine and Bret as two summer-camp counsellors. The episode kicked off Season Twenty-Two of the long-running American show and was first aired in September 2010.

JEMAINE CLEMENT AND BRET
MACKENZIE OF FLIGHT OF THE
CONCHORDS FAME. THE WRITERS OF
THE INBETWEENERS, IAIN MORRIS AND
DAMON BEESLEY, CO-WROTE TWO
EPISODES OF THE CULT COMEDY SHOW.

In total, The Flight of the Conchords have released five albums: *Folk the World Tour*, *The BBC Radio Series: Flight of the Conchords*, *The Distant Future*, *Flight of the Conchords* and *I Told You I Was Freaky*.

In their personal careers, Jemaine has appeared as a voice artist in the animated Hollywood movies *Despicable Me* (2010) and *Rio* (2011) and also acted in the film adaptation of *Dinner for Schmucks* (2010), alongside Steve Carell, Paul Rudd and Zach Galifianakis. In 2012, Jemaine will appear alongside Will Smith and Tommy Lee-Jones in *Men In Black III*, playing the character of Boris.

Bret McKenzie played the role of an elf in *The Lord of the Rings: The Fellowship of the Ring* (2001) and *The Lord of the Rings: The Return of the King* (2003). He is also providing one of the voices for an animated CGI film set in the outback, which is due for release in 2012, starring alongside Tim Curry and Rob Schneider.

Football Friend

Played by the actor Luke Norris, 'Football Friend' appears in Episode Four of Series One. Norris's other appearances include another E4 TV series *Skins* (2009) and the 2008 film *The Duchess* starring Keira Knightley and Ralph Fiennes.

'Fwend' is a term used to describe an outsider to a

group, who is friends with one of the members. It is used in a mocking way and accompanied by a high-pitched voice and two thumbs up. The prefix can be changed according to the situation, and throughout the series different versions of the term have included 'Football Friend', 'Car Friend' and 'Weird Old Inappropriate Friend'.

g is for...

Gilbert, Mr

REPORT CARD

Psychology: A+ – Gilbert has an excellent ability to make his pupils feel like worthless, inadequate morsels.

Biology: B – Experience counts for a lot with this subject and, given his comments about Mrs McKenzie and his looks at Miss Timbs, this is an area where he has a lot of experience!

PE: B – Gilbert keeps an excellent bill of health, thanks to his constant running around to keep Mr Kennedy in check.

History: A+ – As one of the oldies, Gilbert has first-hand knowledge of many of the country's historic events.

Ethics: F – No regard for any other human being, best shown through his treatment of student Will McKenzie.

MR GILBERT IS PLAYED BY COMEDIAN GREG DAVIES.

BACKGROUND

Phil Gilbert is the type of teacher everyone dreads. Head of sixth form at Rudge Park Comp, he hates his job – 'It's not so much a calling these days as a graveyard for the unlucky and the unambitious' – and also the pupils he has to teach. Not only does Gilbert hate kids but he also gets a lot (really a *lot*!) of enjoyment out of watching them squirm, especially Will McKenzie!

From the first episode, he takes a particular dislike to Will. After refusing to listen to Will's input on the school's policy on making new kids wear a badge, he catches Will announcing to the class that Gilbert's a freak who loves sucking the headmaster's balls! Not the best first impression Will could have made. This gives Gilbert all the ammunition he needs and, in the series to follow, he takes every opportunity to get one back on the privately educated know-it-all.

Some of Gilbert's best moments with Will include him threatening his pupil if he grasses on whoever tied him up and put a bin on his head, forcing him to take a work placement at a mechanic's and threatening to ruin his chances of getting into university if he doesn't snitch on the vandals of the local roundabout (Jay and Neil, unsurprisingly!).

FUNNIEST SCENE

After forcing Will to go to a mechanic's for his work experience following a mix-up, Gilbert takes much pleasure in hearing of the week's failings. The guys at the garage throw Will in a lake and, when his mum complains, Gilbert can't help but burst into fits of laughter. After composing himself for a second, he starts up again when Will's mum mentions finding frogspawn in his underpants. Gilbert has to leave the room for another fit of laughter.

LOVES

Polly McKenzie (Will's mum)
Embarrassing pupils
Miss Timbs

HATES

Teaching
Will, Neil, Jay, Simon, school-goers in general
Grasses
When Will calls him 'Phil'
Mr Hopkins (the headmaster)

HOBBIES

As long as it doesn't involve seeing pupils of Rudge Park Comp, Phil Gilbert is easily pleased. He can usually be found at the local shopping centre,

Waterside, looking at teddies or down his local, The Black Horse.

> *Did you know?*
> Actor Greg Davies who plays Mr Gilbert insists on wearing all his own clothes for filming – no padded elbows, although his personal wardrobe does look suspiciously like a real-life teacher's.

Gordon Anderson

British television writer and director Gordon Anderson directed Series One of *The Inbetweeners* in 2008. Before moving on to the small screen, he was a highly acclaimed theatre director, working at the Royal Court Theatre and Royal Shakespeare Company. His first major work was as a TV director on *Suburban Shootout*, a dark comedy which aired in 2006 on Channel 5. Since then he has gone on to write and direct episodes of the BBC hit comedy *The Catherine Tate Show* and ITV's satirical comedy *Moving Wallpaper*. In 2011, he started work on a feature film starring Catherine Tate.

GREG DAVIES AND BLAKE HARRISON DURING FILMING FOR COMIC RELIEF'S RUDE ROAD TRIP.

Greg Davies

Writer, actor and comedian Greg Davies plays Phil Gilbert, head of the sixth form at Rudge Park Comprehensive. He was born in Shropshire on 14 May 1970 and, at 6ft 8 inches, he is surely one of the tallest comedians around.

Davies began his acting career as part of the comedy sketch trio We Are Klang, with Steve Hall and Marek Larwood. It was formed in the early 2000s, with sketches notorious for their rude humour towards both the writers and their audience. After the trio were nominated for, and won, various awards, along with critical acclaim during their time at comedy festivals, *We Are Klang* was commissioned in 2009 by BBC3 and aired for one series. The sitcom was based around three incapable local councillors and was filmed in front of a studio audience.

In 2007, Davies began to forge his way into the comedy circuit and, while continuing his work with We Are Klang, he made several brief appearances on TV comedies, including an episode of *Saxondale*, the comedy series written by and starring Steve Coogan (aka Alan Partridge).

After securing the part of Mr Gilbert for three successful series of *The Inbetweeners*, Davies continued to write and perform. In 2010, he co-wrote and starred in the first series of *Ask Rhod Gilbert*, in which celebrities and members of the public would ask the host comedian Rhod Gilbert a question and they would find out the answer on the show. Throughout 2010, Davies appeared in many panel shows, including *Never Mind The Buzzcocks*, *Have I Got News For You* and *The Graham Norton Show*. In addition to this, he also made a series of online comedy sketches in association with the National Grid Student Union, which aimed to promote the safety and wellbeing of students.

It was during this year that he would start to craft a

path into mainstream comedy and, towards the end of 2010, he appeared in *Live at the Apollo*, a prime-time BBC stand-up comedy show which has been running since 2004. The programme has been a showcase for established comedy acts and also provides a platform for new stand-up comedians. Over the years, many famous faces from the UK and abroad have appeared on *Live at the Apollo*, including Joan Rivers, Jack Dee, Rob Brydon, Jimmy Carr, Michael McIntyre and Frankie Boyle. On Davies' episode, which aired on 9 December 2010, the other comedians to appear were Dara O'Briain and Stewart Francis.

In 2011, he was preparing for his national stand-up tour consisting of 30 dates around the country. The show, entitled 'Firing Cheeseballs at a Dog', was his first solo stand-up tour.

Did you know?
Before playing Mr Gilbert in *The Inbetweeners*, Greg Davies was, in fact, a teacher. He taught Drama and English for 15 years before making his way into comedy.

h is for...

Hawaii Edition

Driving is a massive milestone for any seventeen-year-old, so, when Inbetweener Simon passes his driving test first time round, it's a big deal and his proud parents award this achievement with a new (used) car.

Simon's mum breaks the news: 'It's a Fiat or something, but he [Simon's dad] says it is second-hand.'

Wide-eyed, Simon thanks her in an unusually polite manner: 'Oh my God, Mum – that doesn't matter, this is so cool!'

But his joy quickly turns to disappointment as Simon turns around to see his dad hooting the horn of a banana-yellow Fiat Cinquecento, circa 1996.

Simon's face drops as he realises this isn't a joke and that he's actually going to have to drive the thing! As he checks out its top features (if you can call them that) – a tape deck, sunroof, plastic wheel trims, black bumpers and a 'trendy' paint-job – his initial enthusiasm swiftly dies.

Described by bully Mark Donovan and friends as the 'bender mobile' and a 'paedo's car', things go from bad to worse for Simon's Cinquecento after the yellow passenger door is replaced with a red one following an eventful outing to Thorpe Park.

Some of the best action the yellow rust bucket gets to see includes a trip to London, where the Inbetweeners end up hiding in their car from a crazy man, a visit to Warwick when they have to drive home naked, and Neil's sexual antics with the punk girl at Caravan Club.

In the last episode of Series Three, 'Camping Trip', the car comes to its final resting place when, thanks to Jay and Neil, it rolls into a lake. Although Simon at first flips out at the other Inbetweeners, he comes to realise that maybe the car was a bit shit.

In fact, the guys have revealed in an E4 web chat that filming in the car wasn't always as much fun as it looks. Blake Harrison (Neil) observed that Buckley (Jay) farting in the car was the worst habit of any of the gang. Joe Thomas (Simon) added that Buckley should be put in prison on the grounds that his farts have no place in a civilised society!

> *Did you know?*
> The stylish Hawaii Edition was never actually available to buy and is just a ploy on the part of the Inbetweeners' writers to add even more piss-taking opportunities around the car. So, *Inbetweeners'* fans, sorry to disappoint but you won't find it at your local dodgy second-hand car dealership!

SIMON'S 'BENDER MOBILE' – THE YELLOW FIAT CINQUECENTO, WITH REPLACEMENT DOOR FOLLOWING AN EVENTFUL TRIP TO THORPE PARK.

'Home Alone': Series Three, Episode Five

The episode starts with Jay being left alone in his house for a couple of hours and, like all hormonal male teenagers, he decides that a good old tug is in order – which would usually be fine, if it wasn't for the family dog Benji watching on. As you would, Jay asks his closest friends about the problem of wanking while being observed by the family dog and, as you might expect, they don't have a great deal of sympathy.

Will's mum arrives home and, after being suitably ogled by Jay, Simon and Neil, she announces that she is going away for the weekend with an old friend (Fergus) from college, much to the dismay of Will, who isn't entirely thrilled about her meeting up with a Facebook stalker! However, it's good news for the rest of the lads, especially Neil, who declares that, with Will's mum on Facebook, that's definitely his wank sorted for the night!

On the way home, Jay decides to kick someone's flowerbed for a laugh. Asked if he would like to try it out, Simon doesn't see the funny side, however, and decides he's better off playing golf with his dad in the Father & Son Tournament at the local club. According to Jay, golf stands for 'Gay Outdoor Lifestyle with Fellas' but Simon takes no notice and leaves his friend as he spots a beautiful flower arrangement with the words, 'Welcome to our Village'.

Meanwhile, Will has more pressing matters on his hands now that his mum is going away for the weekend with another man and also that Mr Gilbert has asked Will if he could set him up with his mum! The others have expressed little sympathy and were more interested in when the party would be over the weekend.

Not only is Gilbert interested in a date with Polly McKenzie, he also assigns Will to find out who has vandalised the town's flowerbed to read 'We Come Tit Village'. With Will not present at the time of such loutish behaviour from Neil and Jay, he is genuinely bemused. However, with the prospect of Gilbert messing up his university application if he doesn't find out, he decides to investigate and his first port of call is his two half-wit friends, Neil and Jay, who proudly own up to the crime.

The time has come for Mrs McKenzie's weekend away with Fergus, and Neil has joined Will, together with PS3 and bread for toasting, ready to stay the night. After trying to get rid of his dog Benji, it isn't long before Jay joins the party either – even though Will certainly doesn't want him around due to the threat of him wanking over his mum's knickers! After five minutes of causing chaos, Jay thinks it's time that he takes Will out on the 'pussy patrol' (in other words, a random drive in Jay's mum's car around the neighbourhood, looking for unsuspecting girls to stalk while listening to hardcore gangster rap). As they head round the block, Jay manages to swerve to avoid a passing squirrel and then out of nowhere mysteriously reverses the car in order to hit the innocent creature. 'He's made you look a right mug!' says Neil, as Jay furiously revs the engine to go for a third-time-lucky attempt and this time successfully manages to run over the creature, to his deep regret afterwards: 'His eyes look sad!'

When they finally return home after dealing with the squirrel carcass, they find Simon, golf clubs in tow and suitably attired, waiting for them. But things don't take long to get out of hand again: Jay has the beers delivered on Will's mum's card, Simon changes the profile picture on Will's Facebook page to a fat naked man and Neil blocks the toilet – all in a good ten minutes' work.

After dealing with the blockage, Will finds the rest of the lads outside smashing up his mum's flowers with Simon's golf clubs. 'What the fuck are you doing?' is his natural response and, of course, the reply from Jay is nothing short of pure nonsense: 'They're only daffodils! Fucking little show-offs – "Oh look at me, I'm out first and I'm all yellow!"' The only answer is to get everyone out of the house immediately.

Unfortunately, going out of the house drinking with golf clubs in hand wasn't the best idea and, after they find another flowerbed to attack, it's game on again. Will's apprehension is too much for Jay and he assures him that the flowers will grow back pretty quickly (he knows this because his dad used to shag Delia Smith!). As they all tee off on the flowers in the front garden of one of Will's neighbours, a light appears in an upstairs window and, soon afterwards, it's accompanied by an angry man banging on the window. There's only one thing for it – they run back to the house.

As with all good drinking sessions, the four lads wake the next day to a series of bangs on the front door adding to the inevitable hangovers. The prospect of Simon missing the golf tournament is unfortunately overshadowed by an angry neighbour demanding to know why his flowers have been destroyed so Will talks to him from the safety of his house and tries to reason with him: 'Now, sir, please calm down. I've got a really bad hangover so, if you're not willing to have a sensible conversation, I'm just going to shut the curtains.'

Naturally, this riles the neighbour even more – 'You're taking the fucking high ground with me?' – but the angrier he gets, the calmer Will becomes, as he shuts the curtains.

To add to the confusion, Jay appears upstairs with a more-than-depressed look on his face: 'I've just had a call from my dad – he's had Benji put down,' he tells them and then: 'What have I done? I'll never wank again!' he screams as he breaks down in tears.

While Neil consoles his friend, Will's mum arrives home with a stern look on her face and deals with the angry neighbour. It's been another calamitous weekend, which has landed the foursome in more serious hot water – not to mention a deceased, voyeuristic dog!

Did you know?
In the scene with the squirrel, an actual squirrel trainer was used to train the creature during the shots. He was coaxed in and out of the camera's view by using a nut on a stick.

Hopkins, Mr

The elusive headmaster of Rudge Park Comprehensive –'Mr L. Hopkins MEd' – is never actually seen. In fact, the only glimpse we get of Mr Gilbert's boss is in the first episode, when Will and the other new starters (or 'freaks' as he calls them) are introduced to the school.

There is a deleted scene where Hopkins (played by Martin Ball) does have a small speaking role: 'I think you'll find we're a happy school, this is a bully-free

THE BOYS ALL FANCY WILL'S MUM WHO IS PLAYED BY BELINDA STEWART-WILSON.

zone.' This is where Will finds out that his mum has told the school he's moved because he was being bullied, with Mr Hopkins quoting one of the taunts Will's mum claimed he was subjected to: 'Your dad shags prozzies!' That scene never made the final cut, although Hopkins is referred to throughout the series.

Did you know?
Martin Ball has appeared in a string of British TV shows, including *Doctor Who*, *The Bill* and *Casualty*. He also had a small part in *Ali G Indahouse* (2002).

i is for...

Insults

The insults from the show have become legendary and no doubt replicated in households with hormonal teenagers across the UK. Here are some of the top insults from the Inbetweeners characters:

JAY

Jay is the prince of the Inbetweeners insults, his quick wit and childish banter often impresses Neil, but not so for the likes of Will, who prefers a more sophisticated slur. The majority of Jay's remarks are aimed at Will, mostly because of his preference in the hand baggage department. Will is the easiest of targets for Jay, 'briefcase mong' is one of his favourites, along with 'count spackula' and 'Sponge-Bob shit-his-pants'.

In the 'Duke of Edinburgh Awards' episode, Jay was on fire with insults directed at Will. It all started when Will announced they would be doing voluntary work at an old people's home: 'It's important for you to spend time at an old people's home "cos you're a paedo".' When Will corrected Jay on the specifics of the quip, he came back with another cracker: 'All right, well, you're an O.A.Paedo.' Brilliant.

Later on in the episode, Jay and Neil decide to treat Will to a bit of hair-removal action in the nether regions: 'He's probably only got about four pubes and he pisses through one of them' was the ridiculous comment right before applying the cream. The cream of the crop came in response to Will and the others mounting their challenge to Jay's abuse: 'Say what you like, at least I don't have to wipe old arse just to get a duke of spastic award.'

WILL

Ever the intellect, Will started off his life at Rudge Park Comprehensive insulting the head of sixth form Mr Gilbert: 'I'm such a big huge massive freak, and I just love to suck the headmaster's balls.' Naturally, the comment wasn't well received by Gilbert, who was standing right behind him. Most of Will's insults are as a comeback to Jay's abuse, often aimed at his love of Caravan Club: 'It's a sense of shitting in a bucket that you don't get with other holidays.'

One of Will's strangest insults was directed at a flock of seagulls outside the hostel in Swanage. Out of nowhere when talking to Simon he unleashed a torrent of abuse at the innocent creatures: 'FUCK OFF! You beady-eyed little shits!' Presumably they were after his lunch.

Will's best insults often come during his commentary in between scenes, one of the best ones coming during his date with big Kerry: 'A few years ago I'd seen King Kong at the cinema, now I was on a date with her.'

It's fair to say Will got a barrage of insults thrown at him after his little accident in the exam room, the highlights of those being 'Dr Poo', 'Bum-log millionaire' and 'Vladimir Pootin'.

SIMON

The majority of Simon's insults are focused on Tom, Carli's on-off boyfriend. The abuse is often a criticism of his character and attitude towards Carli, and is delivered in a concise and articulate manner: 'He's a stupid lanky twat, isn't he?'

Simon seems to take a lot of abuse from his friends but he is the master when you catch him on the wrong day, especially around his family: 'I'm not spending another second in this house with you utter twats.' His parents frequently take the brunt of his abuse, and the comments are usually delivered behind their backs, for example when assuring Tara his mum definitely won't be at the Failsafe gig: 'She won't be there, stupid bitch.' Or when fuming at his dad for moving the family to Swansea, he lashed out again: 'He's in his fucking forties, his life is practically over.'

Simon's most peculiar insult was very much directed towards himself. When spending a night with Tara in Warwick, Simon attempted to coax his 'flaccid' penis out of its cage: 'Just work, you stupid fucking thing, get big!'

During the final episode, Simon reached boiling point, firstly, when a defenceless dinner lady distracted him when he wanted to catch up with the love of his life: 'That stupid ugly bitch just ruined it for me,' and, secondly, when Jay and Neil allowed his car to roll into the lake for no apparent reason: 'I've wasted my life hanging around with you fucking morons!' However, after a few minutes of flapping around in the water, Simon was back to his normal grumpy self.

NEIL

Neil's insults often arrive when he doesn't realise it, let alone anyone else! They often come in the form of backhanded compliments or just downright stupidity. For example, Neil's view on wheelchair-bound Alistair Scott: 'He was always a bit lazy though.'

Similarly to Jay, Neil directs his insults at soft-touch Will: 'Won't university be a bit boring? Just a load of "Wills" hanging around?' Neil's fascination with Will's background goes way beyond his time at Rudge Park Comprehensive: 'Is this like a posho's tradition? Did your mates do the same for you when you were at Hogwarts?'

Neil's insults are simple and straight to the point. If we were to sum his insults up, it would be at his eighteenth birthday party when asking Will if he had brought along his girlfriend Kerry: 'Is big foot here?'

TERRY CARTWRIGHT

If Jay is the prince of insults, then his dad Terry is most definitely the king. Most, if not all, of his insults are directed at his son in a cruel and patronising manner. 'Jay's about as much use as a nun's tits.' What a great way to build your child's confidence.

The insults flow like wine when Terry is around, especially to embarrass Jay in front of his friends: 'You definitely take after your mum in the cock-sized department, she ain't got one either.'

Surely the most shocking of all insults comes in the caravan, which seems to be the place where Terry gets most of his inspiration: 'The only pussy he's ever touched was his mum's when he fell out of it.' Terry Cartwright, you beautiful man!

GENERAL INSULTS

Insults are the name of the game around Rudge Park Comp, and you'll be lucky not to walk down the corridors without hearing the words 'Wanker!', 'Boner!' or 'What a spastic badge!' No doubt if you bump into Mark Donovan, you're bound to get some ill-treatment along the lines of 'Here they are, team twat' or 'What the fuck are you two queers doing?!'

However, if you're a student in Rudge Park, it's good to know the head of sixth form Mr Gilbert is there to give you total support and encouragement during your time in school: 'Good morning, and shut up!'

In 2009, Joe Thomas and Simon Bird from the show produced a guide to insulting your mates on an ITN online broadcast. Some of the tips they gave included insulting someone's mum, turning anything into an innuendo and insulting someone when they show the slightest chink of vulnerability!

Did you know?
'rzucaj sobie w kogos innego, idiota! slepy jestes?! otworz oczy!' The insult an angry Polish girl threw towards Will in Episode Two. It happens when Will throws the Frisbee at a girl in the wheelchair. The angry insult directed at Will is literally translated as *'Throw yourself in someone else, idiot! Are you blind?! Open your eyes!'*

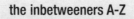

Jay Cartwright, played by James Buckley, is the prince of Inbetweeners insults.

j is for...

James Buckley (Jay)

BACKGROUND

James Patrick Buckley is best known for his foul-mouthed portrayal of Jay Cartwright in *The Inbetweeners*. Born in 1987, in Croydon, Greater London, it didn't take him long to get a taste for performing and, while attending the Beam Primary School in Dagenham, Essex, he discovered his love of acting while taking part in school plays. At just seven years old, James took it one step further and started to attend stage school at weekends.

It was only four years until he made his first break into

JAMES BUCKLEY
WITH GIRLFRIEND
CLAIR MEEK.

acting, aged eleven, when he got a part in the West End show *Whistle Down the Wind*, followed by *Les Misérables*.

While he was studying at Colin's Performing Arts School in Essex, one of Buckley's classmates was British singer and songwriter (and Brit Awards winner) Jessie J. She also performed alongside him in *Whistle Down the Wind*. In an interview with the *Sun*, Jessie explained how even then *The Inbetweeners'* star was known for his comedy antics: 'James was a right laugh! He was the naughty one with all the cheek in classes.'

He later went on to make a string of TV appearances in popular shows such as *The Bill*, *Holby City*, *Skins* and *Teachers* before his big break in *The Inbetweeners* in 2008. In March 2011, he was nominated for the Royal Television Society 'Comedy Performance' Award for *The Inbetweeners*, but was beaten to the accolade by Miranda Hart for her self-titled BBC sitcom, *Miranda*.

James Buckley is signed to Lisa Thomas Management alongside some of the UK's best comedy performers, including John Bishop and Mackenzie Crook (*The Office*). His best-known show since *The Inbetweeners* is BBC's *Rock & Chips*, the prequel to the British comedy institution *Only Fools and Horses*. Set in the 1960s and originally named *Sex, Drugs, Rock & Chips*, it tells the story of Joan and Reg Trotter and their teenage son

Derek (or 'Del-Boy'), played by Buckley. The prequel explores the story of Joan and Reg's strained relationship and the events leading up to Joan's affair with Freddie 'The Frog' Robdal, resulting in the birth of Del's younger brother, Rodney.

Although the show received mixed reviews from the critics, there was much praise for Buckley's involvement, with Paul Whitelaw of the *Scotsman* saying that the actor 'delivered a charming performance', admitting that, although he was playing the famous 'Del-Boy', it was 'effectively a supporting role'. Meanwhile, Keith Watson in the *Metro* said of Buckley and Bright (Joan Trotter, Del-Boy's mother), 'They deserved a show all to themselves.'

Talking to the BBC, James explained what working on the project meant to him: 'It was a dream come true and a great opportunity for me.'

The next project was the BBC's *Off The Hook*, originally titled *Fresh* when it aired as five short online episodes. *Off The Hook* is a sitcom focusing on the lives of a group of freshers starting at the fictional Bankside University. The series follows the student adventures of Danny Gordon (played by Jonathan Bailey) and his best friend Shane (Danny Morgan), along with friends including Fred (James Buckley). Despite the show being compared to *The Inbetweeners*, Buckley's character couldn't be more different to Jay Cartwright. Fred is a depressed, dry and totally unenthused character consumed with thoughts of 'impending death' – best seen in Season One, Episode Two through his song, 'What's the Point?':

WHAT'S THE POINT OF WAKING UP?
WHAT'S THE POINT IN GETTING OUT OF BED?
WHAT'S THE POINT OF ANYTHING WHEN
WE'RE ALL GOING TO END UP DEAD?

Outside of acting, James Buckley is a big music fan. He can be seen showing off his guitar skills in the 'Rude Road Trip' in the back of the infamous yellow Fiat. It was reported in the *Sun* that he has taken his skills one step further after making a guest appearance on Steve Craddock's (Ocean Colour Scene) solo album. The pair reportedly met at the band's anniversary gig in London and agreed to work together after revealing they're massive fans of each other's work.

Did you know?
James Buckley set himself a personal challenge to try to get a wink in every episode but because the scenes are filmed out of order, he ended up winking a lot to try to make sure it worked!

Jay Cartwright

REPORT CARD

Creative Writing: A – Jay is very imaginative with his stories.

History: D – Doesn't look into the past much and doesn't want anybody to know about his childhood.

Sex Education: A+ – Jay takes an active role in class, always listens and helps others out.

English: C – Jay's language is very colourful but could be a little cleaner.

Drama: B – Can put on a very impressive show, but only in front of friends.

BACKGROUND

It's fair to say that everyone knows someone like Jay, the serial bullshitter who loves to take the piss out of everyone, during school years. Added to that, his obsession with sex is bordering on scary, his tales of romps with lesbian twins and models seem to impress Neil but not so much Will or Simon who are wise to them and often ignore his constant wittering.

Jay is very much a complex character: around his friends, he will often put on a front but you'll regularly catch a glimpse of his vulnerability. That weakness frequently becomes apparent in scenes with his dad, in the scenes with his girlfriend Chloe (Series Two) or when he is left alone in the London club without the safety net of having Neil around.

FUNNIEST SCENE

Jay is often the provider of the majority of comedic moments when the four lads are around; however, one of the funniest scenes came about from Jay speaking to an outsider. Much to the other's confusion, he explains that he is an old friend and they both had trials at West Ham. After that, Jay's friend becomes more commonly known as 'Football Fwend'. Putting that phrase together with two thumbs up really riles Jay, so, when Jay, Neil and Simon spot 'Football Fwend's' car outside his house, it's an ideal opportunity to take the piss. After that, Jay decides enough is enough and out of nowhere starts to jump on the bonnet of his car, shouting, 'Friend, friend, fucking football friend, you're not my fucking friend, all right!'

LOVE INTERESTS

If you were to believe everything Jay tells you, he got his first blowjob at the age of twelve from the cleaner and it's a well-known fact that Caravan Club is like a sex club all over Europe. However, at the end of Series Two, he actually finds a girlfriend by the name of Chloe, who seems to bring out more of his sensitive side, but, after finding out that she may have got off with one of the other lads in school, he starts to become suspicious. Not knowing what to do, he takes advice from none other than his dad, who tells him that the only way to find out what she's up to is to know where she is all the time. After 14 texts a day, along with other social media channels, Chloe decides he's far too intense for her and dumps Jay outside the pub, leaving him in tears.

LOVES

Taking the piss out of his friends
Bullshitting
Dutch girls

HATES

His dad taking the piss
Old people
People waiting at the bus stops

HOBBIES

Caravan clubbing in Camber Sands – it gives Jay the sense of freedom you just don't get with other holidays, plus the caravan 'clunge' is some of the best (according to the serial bullshitter).

> *Did you know?*
> In the scene where Jay crashes Neil's motorbike, a stunt man played the part of Jay. If you look closely when he rides past the camera, the stunt man looks considerably older and a lot different than Jay!

Joe Thomas

Simon Cooper in the hit series is played by Joe Thomas, who was born on 28 October 1983 in Chelmsford, Essex.

After finishing school, Joe went on to study at Cambridge University, where he met his co-star Simon Bird and writing partner Jonny Sweet. During his time at Cambridge, he joined Footlights, the theatrical club whose alumni boast an impressive list

of British comedy greats. It was at Footlights where all three went on to write and perform in the national tour 'Niceties' (2006), a sketch show that would garner critical acclaim and set them up for a future in comedy.

Thomas and Sweet took their two-man show to London's Fringe Festival and would constantly write and perform together during their time at Cambridge. They took part in 'Project V', an online-based comedy show, and also have their own comedy channel on the social networking site Myspace. At the time of writing, it is believed that Thomas, Sweet and Bird have been working on other TV and film projects.

It was those performances with Sweet and Bird that got Thomas noticed on the comedy scene and it wasn't long before he and Bird became friends with Iain Morris and Damon Beesley, writers of *The Inbetweeners*. After an invitation to audition for the role of Simon Cooper, Joe was awarded the part.

After *The Inbetweeners'* third series, he worked as a writer on Simon Bird's BBC3 comedy *The King is Dead*, and co-wrote the episode 'Assistant Regional Head of Sales' (which aired on 23 September 2010), where Eamonn Holmes walks away victorious.

Opposite: Joe Thomas plays Simon.

> *Did you know?*
> Joe has been dating Hannah Tointon, his co-star in
> *The Inbetweeners*. Hannah (Tara) has also appeared in
> *Hollyoaks* and is the sister of former *EastEnders* actress
> and *Strictly Come Dancing* winner Kara Tointon.

Jonny Sweet

English actor, writer and comedian Jonny Sweet is from
Nottingham and was born in 1985. His connection
with *The Inbetweeners* began when he met Simon Bird
and Joe Thomas at Cambridge University. It was there
that they would start a writing team performing
sketches at the famous Footlights amateur dramatics
theatre. In 2007, the three took their show to the
Edinburgh Comedy Festival to much acclaim.
However, when the others went off to film *The
Inbetweeners*, Sweet went solo and, in 2009, he received
the award of Best Newcomer in Edinburgh for his
performance in the play *Mostly About Arthur*. His major
TV roles have come on Channel 4 and he is particularly
noted for playing Prime Minister David Cameron in
the More4 mock documentary *When Boris Met Dave*.
Since then, he has taken his one-man show *Let's Just All
Have Some Fun (And Learn Something for Once)* to sell-
out audiences and five-star reviews.

After Sweet made a cameo appearance in *The Inbetweeners* as Dean in the 'Night Out in London' episode, along with Bird and Thomas he had a pilot for a new sitcom commissioned for Channel 4 in late 2010. The trio will write and star in *Chickens*, a story about three men who try to dodge their National Service during World War I. Kenton Allen, chief executive of Big Talk Productions (the company

HANNAH TOINTON AND JOE THOMAS FILMING 'THE GIG AND THE GIRLFRIEND' EPISODE FOR SERIES THREE. THE PAIR ARE REPORTEDLY DATING OFF-SCREEN AS WELL.

handling the show), spoke glowingly about the young comedians: 'I've seen the future of comedy, and I'm afraid to say it's Simon, Joe and Jonny shaped. They are a delight to work with, have razor-sharp comedy minds and *Chickens* promises to be very special indeed.'

K is for...

Katie Sutherland

Neil's unbelievably fit sister Katie Sutherland lives with her brother, along with her dad and mechanic boyfriend (who never makes an appearance). She first appears in the sitcom in the trip to London episode, when the guys go round to Neil's expecting a lift in his new car. When she opens the door to Simon, Jay and Will, they are completely besotted by the sight of her revealing cleavage, so much so that she has to ask them nicely to refrain: 'Can you please stop looking at my tits?' Her other appearance in the show comes in Series Three at Neil's eighteenth birthday party and once again her revealing clothing has the four guys somewhat distracted.

Katie Sutherland is played by Kacey Barnfield, who was born on 14 January 1988. Before *The Inbetweeners*, her acting career took off as a youngster with

KACEY BARNFIELD PLAYS
NEIL'S 'UNBELIEVABLY FIT'
OLDER SISTER, KATIE

appearances in the long-running BBC children's drama series *Grange Hill*, after which she moved on to other famous British TV series such as *The Bill* and *Casualty*. Her biggest role to date came in late 2010 with the part of Crystal Waters in the Hollywood movie *Resident Evil: Afterlife*, a film made off the back of several prequels and made famous by a video game in the early 1990s.

In her personal life, Kacey has been dating England all-round cricketer Stuart Broad since 2009.

Did you know?
Kacey is second cousin to fellow actress Victoria Shalet, who is famous for playing the role of Melody in the CBBC series *The Queen's Nose*.

Kennedy, Mr 'Paedo'

REPORT CARD

Music: F – After being caught in the music cupboard touching himself, it was a certain fail.

PE: F – Following a field trip that involved Kennedy supplying a pupil with his trunks, he could only receive an F.

Art and Design: F – Kennedy was overly enthusiastic to help out at the school fashion show.

BACKGROUND

First introduced in Series Two, Mr Kennedy is Rudge Park's resident paedo. The rumours about Mr Kennedy started after he was allegedly caught one day in the music cupboard pleasuring himself over the orchestra and so the affectionate nickname 'Paedo Kennedy' was born.

It's on the Swanage field trip where Kennedy's criminal profile is heightened, after he bargains with Neil to allow him on the trip if Neil agrees to be his 'special helper'. Ever the unaware, Neil obviously agrees to this transparent ploy and, despite the fact that he doesn't take any of the classes related to the trip, he joins in as Kennedy's assistant.

Once on the trip, Kennedy's motives become obvious as Neil explains to the others that he went swimming with Mr Kennedy in budgie smugglers he had kindly provided in exchange for a bottle of vodka. Despite Will being appalled at this clear case of grooming, the Inbetweeners decide they're happy to pimp Will out to the suspected paedophile, if it means easy access to booze.

Later that night, Mr Gilbert finds Kennedy in the boys' room, trying to give Neil a leg massage to help him relax after the swimming. Gilbert seems aware of the rumours about Kennedy and quickly shepherds him away. This is seen again in a later episode – 'The

Fashion Show' – when Kennedy once again takes a liking to Neil, much to everyone else's amusement. When Gilbert finds Kennedy trying to get Neil changed, he forces him away once more – although this time he reveals that he can't keep putting his neck on the line for him. After this incident, Paedo Kennedy is never seen again.

FUNNIEST SCENE

Kennedy's funniest scene is during the Rudge Park fashion show when he is the only teacher to offer to help out in the dressing area. When Kennedy sees Neil, his eyes light up and he tries to help him undress. Even when Neil tells him that he's not even in the show, the teacher carries on until Mr Gilbert comes to Neil's rescue.

LOVES

Neil Sutherland
Swimming with Neil Sutherland
Massaging Neil Sutherland's legs
Giving Neil Sutherland the thumbs-up

HATES

Mr Gilbert interrupting his alone time with Neil

HOBBIES

Kennedy loves a swim in the sea with his favourite pupil, Neil Sutherland.

> *Did you know?*
> There is actually a Facebook group dedicated to Mr 'Paedo' Kennedy. At the time of writing, the group has 1,780 members. The group contains his best quotes from the show posted by its members, and a profile picture of him giving two thumbs up.

Kerry

Otherwise known as 'Big Kerry', she appears in the 'Will's Dilemma' episode, where Simon arranges a double date with his girlfriend Tara and Kerry, one of Tara's taller-than-average friends. After Will finds out that Kerry has given blowjobs to her last three boyfriends, he decides to string her along somewhat in order to get his share. Eventually, he calls off the 'relationship', which finished with him being thrown out of Neil's birthday party and Kerry in floods of tears. Kerry is played by Abbey Mordue, who has mostly worked in theatre during her career; two highlights being *Jerry Springer The Opera* and *Oliver's Army* in 2009. Despite her massive appearance on *The*

Inbetweeners, Abbey is, in fact, 5ft 11 inches – tall, but no giant!

KEVIN & PERRY GO LARGE

From the moment *The Inbetweeners'* movie was announced in early 2011, critics started to make comparisons with the 2000 comedy *Kevin & Perry Go Large*. Based on the character of Kevin the Teenager from *Harry Enfield and Chums*, the film follows Kevin

THE CAST ARE JOINED BY KATIE PRICE, WHO PRESENTED THEM WITH THEIR VARIETY CLUB AWARD.

(Harry Enfield) and best mate Perry (Kathy Burke) as they go on holiday to Ibiza, where they plan to lose their virginity.

Despite the popularity of the original sketch, it received mixed reviews at the box office, something Simon Bird (Will) is only too keen to avoid, as he told *ShortList*: 'I don't think there's anyone more aware of the fact that the idea of *The Inbetweeners* doing a British feature film might receive a critical beating.

'It's like the *Kevin & Perry* factor. Everyone involved in the film is aware of that and we're doing all we can to make sure no self-respecting critic could write a bad thing about it.'

Comparisons are easy to see, but *The Inbetweeners* has something *Kevin & Perry* didn't: thanks to the three preceding series, it has had long enough to establish the characters and each of their stories. *Kevin & Perry Go Large* had to expand on the original characters from the sketches, whereas *The Inbetweeners*' movie is more of a continuation of the foursome's exploits and the next big stage of their lives: the end of schooldays.

Kevin Sutherland

Neil's Dad, Kevin Sutherland, lives at home with Neil, Neil's sister Katie and Katie's boyfriend, Dave. He is often the subject of taunts about his sexuality due to his

EMILY ATACK ENJOYS A NIGHT OUT WITH HER SISTER MARTHA.

wife leaving him, his love of badminton and general camp mannerisms. Neil frequently endures abuse from his friends regarding his dad's homosexuality, in particular in the 'Bunk Off' episode when Will calls him a 'BUMDER' to his face in a drunken rage. Later in the same episode, when being reprimanded by both sets of parents, Will and Simon accused Kevin of paedophilia when they point to places on a doll where he has touched them. Naturally, Kevin refutes the claims. There has never been any evidence of Kevin's sexuality in the show; however, this doesn't stop the boys (and also their parents) from assuming he is that way inclined.

Kevin Sutherland is played by the English actor Alex MacQueen. His comedy background stems from hit Channel 4 shows *The IT Crowd* and *Peep Show*, along with BBC series *Miranda* and *Come Fly With Me*. In 2010, he reunited with *Inbetweeners'* co-star Blake Harrison in *The Increasingly Poor Decisions of Todd Margaret*. He has also played a number of serious parts, most notably 75 episodes of the BBC hospital drama *Holby City*. Alex MacQueen's film credits include *Four Lions*, a controversial Chris Morris comedy based on four British Muslims.

WRITERS IAIN MORRIS AND DAMON BEESLEY COLLECT THEIR BRITISH COMEDY AWARD.

Did you know?
The character of Neil's dad originates from the mind of writer Damon Beesley, who used to call one of his friends' dads gay. Damon still keeps in touch with his friend and, when the shows first aired, he texted Damon to say, 'My dad plays badminton on a Tuesday, not a Wednesday!'

I is for...

Lauren Harris

Appearing in 'The Field Trip' episode, Lauren takes an initial liking to Will on the bus to Swanage but then becomes more interested in Simon, following Will's weird Yoda impressions and clingy behaviour. Lauren only appears in this episode as it is mentioned that she moves away afterwards. She is played by Jayne Wisener, an actress and singer from Northern Ireland: her first big break came playing Johanna in *Sweeney Todd: The Demon Barber of Fleet Street* (2007) starring Johnny Depp. After her appearance in *The Inbetweeners*, she had

JAYNE WISENER PLAYS LAUREN HARRIS, WHO APPEARS IN THE EPISODE 'THE FIELD TRIP'.

a recurring role in the BBC drama *Casualty*. In 2011, Wisener played the part of Bessie in the hotly anticipated period film drama *Jane Eyre*.

LOCATIONS

School to the Inbetweeners, Rudge Park Comprehensive is the location for many of the hit show's best scenes. It's where the series begins, with Will, following his departure from a lavish private school and it's the location of the famous sixth-form leavers' ball.

The real location for Rudge Park Comp is Ruislip High School, West London. Writers of the show Damon Beesley and Iain Morris chose the establishment apparently due to its intimidating architecture. Eagle-eyed fans will have noticed that in Series One many of the pupils in the background of school scenes are much younger than the Inbetweeners themselves. In fact, lots of them were only in Year 7 and they are the real pupils of Ruislip High School, which had only recently opened. To make sure the Inbetweeners didn't stand out as being much older than all the other pupils, actors were also used in school scenes, particularly in the common room, to giving the school a more college-like feel.

Ruislip High mostly featured in the first series as a mock-up of the common room and other areas of the school built for use in the following series. This was constructed in an abandoned army barracks, where the guys filming had to drink cold water before every take, as the barracks were so cold, you could see their breath on-camera.

'London': Series Two, Episode Four

When the boys tire of life in suburban England, they decide to take a trip to the bright lights of the capital. Jay playing porn videos on his laptop in the sixth-form room doesn't help matters, causing Will to decide enough is enough and it's time for them to try to carve out a name for themselves. 'Carpe Diem' was the cry from the briefcase one – unfortunately for Neil, this doesn't mean a fishing trip so he has to settle on London.

Neil announces he has a car and has passed his test. Finally, Jay no longer has to ride in Simon's little 'bitch mobile', so they all agree Neil will drive them to London for a night's clubbing. Simon, a nervous wreck as usual, is worried about the dangers of the city's mean streets and also, being underage, concerned about not getting into any clubs. Luckily, Jay manages to calm those fears as he goes to London all the time: in fact, in his words, he 'fucked a girl in the Tower of London only

last week!' Asked if she had seen the Crown Jewels, he gave the inevitable response: 'She'd already seen the Crown Jewels, thanks – my bell-end!'

As you might expect, Jay's complete and utter tripe doesn't do anything for Simon's worries, but as they stroll through the school corridors they bump into Carli and her friend, who express an interest in a night out in London, therefore Simon has to go. As a bonus, Carli's friend Rachel also seems to take an interest in Will – well, according to Neil's theory of 'body-language speak', as she touches her hair while talking to him.

When Saturday rolls around, there is plenty to be excited about and Simon has bought some brand-new trainers ready for the prospect of meeting up with Carli. This doesn't go down too well with Will as he specifically requested they all wear smart shoes to get into the top London clubs. It's quickly overlooked, however, as the others mock Will's massive Italian 'flipper' shoes.

Arriving at Neil's house, they are greeted at the door by his incredibly fit sister Katie wearing a very revealing negligee, which has them all transfixed. When Neil comes out to spoil the fun, he shows them his new car complete with body kit and a 'Porsche Engineering' sticker – which Jay describes as a tractor beam for 'fanny'. When Neil is asked how fast the tractor beam goes, he reveals the car doesn't actually have an engine! So again, Simon has to bite the bullet, and drives everyone there in the Fiat after all.

As they set off on their journey, the intellectual conversation starts with talk of 'Who's the fittest?' out of Neil's sister and Will's mum – a unanimous decision proves impossible so Jay tests out another form of banter. In one of the fans' favourite moments from the show, Jay leans out of the car window and shouts 'Bus Wankers!' at a group of unsuspecting victims by a bus stop, much to the delight of the others inside the car.

As often happens with long beer-drinking journeys, Neil needs a pit stop, but, with Simon unwilling to pull over to let him out, he has to use a beer can instead. Much to Simon's annoyance, Neil assures him this will be 'no problemo' and he has it under control. Unfortunately, it's quite the opposite and Neil's pissing spirals out of control. As he strategically tries to change cans, the unthinkable happens as he cuts his manhood: 'Oh shit, my helmet – I've cut it on the can!' It's another great start to an Inbetweeners' road trip.

Approaching the bright lights of London, they seem to spend the majority of their time looking around for a parking space and so, to alleviate the boredom, Jay thinks it's an ideal time for another round of 'Bus Wankers'. Unlike in their quiet hometown, however, London's congestion catches up with them... as do a couple of rather large-looking bus stoppers! Simon is on the receiving end of a throttling and makes a very scared apology so they are let off lightly. 'I'd rather be a Bus Wanker than drive that yellow piece of shit!' is the comment as the two giant characters leave the scene. Lesson learned.

Eventually, the lads find a rather sketchy-looking parking space. Simon is unwilling to park there due to the threat of clamping, but is convinced by the others that this is an unlikely event and if they spend more time looking to park that leaves less time with Carli and Rachel in the club. Added to that, it seems Neil has a 'big problemo' with his knob and therefore they must move at once.

So, after an eventful trip, the lads find the queue to the club and, with some arrogance, push into the section where Carli and Rachel are standing, much to the anger of people waiting behind them, who begin to shout obscenities. 'Get to the back of the queue, you four-eyed prick!' is not an ideal backdrop for Will to begin wooing Rachel. As they make their way to the front, the doorman says the inevitable words feared by Will: 'No trainers!' Even with Simon's plea that they are brand, spanking new, they are denied entry. However, it's not very often a saviour comes in the form of a tramp but tonight seems to be Simon's lucky night, so he borrows piss-smelling shoes from a homeless man –

yes, a homeless man – in exchange for his new trainers and £20, of course.

Unbelievably, it works and they enter the club (or, as Jay refers to it, 'clunge heaven'). As Neil and Jay explore the pulling opportunities, Simon and Will set about finding Carli and Rachel. Simon doesn't make the best impression when he meets Carli on the edge of the dance floor because the stench of urine from the tramp's shoes is unbearable: 'Simon, I'm not being rude, but I think that smell might be you!' And, when Simon confesses, the story doesn't go down like the Shakespearean tale he had hoped for. Will is having similar difficulties with Rachel, the main problem being she has no interest whatsoever in him. Hardly the ideal start to their relationship!

Meanwhile, Neil's 'problemo' has gathered pace in the toilets but, as he tries to fix it, the bouncers steam in and accuse him of something untoward. 'I wasn't wanking! My cock's cut, my cock is cut!' is the cry as Neil is thrown out of the club. It's only fair to say that it was time to leave, anyway!

As they walk back to the car to go home, Simon's fears about the parking space are confirmed when they find a clamp on the car in the same colour as the paintwork. Not only that, but an angry Londoner is waiting there and demands £200 to release the clamp. 'I think you've got a big problemo,' observes Neil.

There's only one thing for it: Simon's dad to the rescue!

Louise Graham

Played by Isabella Laughland, Louise Graham is a girl in the same year as the Inbetweeners at Rudge Park Comprehensive. In Episode Three of Series Two, she hosts a party at her house on the same night as Will's dinner party. Much to Will's dismay, the lads decide to ditch the dinner party and try to get into Louise's house instead. After failing to get through the front door in the conventional way, they feel the next best option is either to scale the fence or climb through dog shit underneath! Following her debut television appearance on *The Inbetweeners*, Isabella Laughland made her way on to the big screen playing Leanne in *Harry Potter and the Half-Blood Prince* (2009), and, in 2011, she portrayed the same character in *Harry Potter and the Deathly Hallows*.

Love Life

Love is not a word you will hear *The Inbetweeners* use very often – unless it's followed by 'muff', 'clunge' or 'Will's mum', it doesn't enter their vocabulary. However, the same cannot be said for the actors who play the comedy foursome.

Joe Thomas (Simon) told the *Sun* that his rise to fame hasn't done much for his pulling power. Similarly to his character, who always struggles when trying to impress Carli D'Amato, the love of his life, Joe admits to failure when it comes to talking to women: 'I use the worst chat-up lines. At university, I said to a girl: "Before I met you, all I could think about was history, now all I can think about is you."' With lines like that, it's no wonder he didn't impress!

He added that despite his fame his luck doesn't seem to have changed: 'I haven't really cashed the TV cheque – I'd worry I couldn't carry it off, being a celebrity.'

Despite his inability to talk to the opposite sex, Joe has managed to pull actress Hannah Tointon, who played his onscreen girlfriend Tara in the second series.

Simon Bird (Will) took it one step further in an interview with the *Sun*. Where Joe thinks he's not cool enough to use his new status as a way of talking to women, Simon said, 'I'm always told, "You're such a pathetic loser in the show, no girl would ever go out with you!"' That's never a good look for anyone. Hopefully, the movie will have added some more cred to his character (although it's highly doubtful!).

Unlike his co-stars, Blake Harrison (Neil) seems to have had no problem impressing the ladies. Blake has a long-term girlfriend: Kerry Ann Lynch. The couple are always talking on Twitter, even posting up pictures of the two of them having dinner.

He does admit, however, that his girlfriend likes to draw a line between himself and his character Neil. 'My girlfriend says I don't look like Neil. I think she says it

JOE THOMAS HAS ADMITTED THAT HIS RISE TO FAME HASN'T REALLY HELPED HIS LOVE LIFE.

to justify to her friends dating someone who is very stupid on TV.'

Through his way with the ladies, Blake has even managed to help out a fan. Someone stopped Blake to ask if he would convince his girlfriend to accept his marriage proposal. Blake kindly obliged by writing a recommendation of the fan for his girlfriend and told her he sounds like a good man.

During filming for the *Inbetweeners'* movie, James Buckley could also be seen to be lucky in love. During a break in filming, Buckley was 'papped' by the *Mirror* embracing his girlfriend Clair Meek and catching a cheeky kiss. What a job!

m is for...

Mark Donovan

REPORT CARD

Art: A+ – Mark has shown great artistic potential in his art project with William McKenzie titled 'Hello! I'm Will and I'm doing a shit'.

PE: A – Excellent at all martial arts and boxing, which is surprising as the school doesn't teach these disciplines.

French: F – After beating up a French exchange student, Mark was dropped from this subject.

Chemistry: B – Has shown great promise in this area, even creating herbal medication out of a teabag.

Design and Technology: B – Created a very useful protective hat in a project with Will McKenzie.

BACKGROUND

Mark Donovan is Rudge Park Comprehensive's resident bully. From the first episode of the show, he takes a particular dislike to Will and climbs up the cubicle where Will is taking a dump to snap a photo of him. The image is then plastered up all over the school with the words: 'Hello! I'm Will and I'm doing a shit'. It's probably not the first impression Will wanted to make, but it's just the start of Donovan's attacks. Throughout the series, his personal attacks on Will continue and include tying him to a chair with a bin on his head.

Sometimes, we do see a different side to Donovan, though. Whenever he's in front of parents, he puts on a highly convincing 'nice guy' act and goes all polite and kind. The biggest difference, however, is when he's around his ex-girlfriend Charlotte 'Big Jugs' Hinchcliffe.

It's obvious he still has feelings for Charlotte and this is partly why he hates Will so much. When he catches Charlotte and Will kissing in the first series, we see another side to Donovan as he tells Will to 'be nice to her because she is kind, fragile and gentle. If you tell anyone I said that, I will kill you!'

Later in the series, he shows his protective side again. When Will catches Patrice and Charlotte upstairs at a party, he points Donovan their way. It's later revealed that Donovan beats up Patrice.

FUNNIEST SCENE

Donovan's most amusing scene is his very first one of the show. While Will's taking a school dump, Donovan and his mate climb over the cubicle and take pictures of Will mid-poo, before posting them all over the school.

LOVES

Charlotte Hinchcliffe
Polly McKenzie
Beating up French exchange students

HATES

Will McKenzie
Simon, Neil and Jay (although his hatred for all three is nothing compared to his feelings towards Will)

HOBBIES

Mark Donovan likes to keep fit. He finds the best form of exercise is running and he keeps it up as part of his daily routine. Rather than paying expensive gym membership, Donovan prefers to do his running when he's chasing bully victims around the school and the local area. He's even been known to use a cricket bat as part of his routine (probably for cardiovascular training on his upper body).

Donovan also likes to dabble in recreational drugs. Contrary to popular belief, he doesn't actually sell drugs but instead prefers to sell the contents of a well-known brand of teabag. Guess the profit margins are much better in tea!

Did you know?
Henry Lloyd-Hughes, the actor who played Mark Donovan, had a minor role as Roger Davies, a Quidditch chaser and captain in *Harry Potter and the Goblet of Fire* (2005). Compared to Hogwarts, Rudge Park Comp must have been a big culture shock!

HENRY LLOYD-HUGHES (CENTRE), SHOWN HERE IN 'PUNK ROCK' AT THE LYRIC THEATRE IN LONDON, PLAYS RUDGE PARK'S RESIDENT BULLY MARK DONOVAN.

Martin Trenaman

You may know Martin best for his role as Alan Cooper (Simon's dad) in *The Inbetweeners*, but he's also appeared as salesman Lance in the hit E4 show *PhoneShop*, as well as in several smaller roles.

Trenaman's character Lance is store manager of the fictitious mobile-phone store. A man stuck in the daily grind, Lance has seen all those around him move on to bigger and better things. Despite this, he still shows passion for his job, mainly because it's an escape from his wife. Following the imprisonment of the store's assistant manager 'Little Gary Patel', Lance hires a graduate called Christopher (Tom Bennett), whom the show follows.

The majority of his TV credits come from his work as a writer. He's written for a variety of comedy programmes including *Never Mind The Buzzcocks*, *The Big Fat Quiz of the Year* and numerous *Comedy Roasts*. In addition, he has written material for comedians including Harry Enfield, Johnny Vaughan and Bill Bailey. No wonder he's so funny as Si's dad!

MARTIN TRENAMAN PLAYS SIMON'S FATHER, ALAN.

Did you know?

Martin Trenaman auditioned for *The Inbetweeners* just two days before the first day of shooting. He was actually in the first scene ever filmed for the show, outside a suit-hire shop before the Xmas Prom. Trenaman was hired on short notice after the original actor pulled out.

Matt Smith

During the gruelling casting process for the first series of *The Inbetweeners*, Matt Smith (best known for his portrayal of the lead in the BBC's legendary *Doctor Who*) auditioned for the show.

Writer Iain Morris told *Digital Spy* that the now famous actor got down to the last ten in the audition process for the part of Will McKenzie. He revealed that Smith was only turned down because he was too

MATT SMITH GOT DOWN TO THE LAST TEN IN THE AUDITION PROCESS FOR THE PART OF WILL.

dashing and more of a heroic leading man – something the character of Will definitely isn't!

Morris added that Simon Bird hit the spot – showing the vulnerability within Will's character while maintaining the humour at the centre of the show. He proved a winning combination for the makers and audience of the show alike!

Merchandise

There's lots of fantastic *Inbetweeners'* merchandise out there! From T-shirts and posters to coffee mugs, the World Wide Web has an array of goods displaying some of the show's famous quotes. The most popular comedy T-shirts include the word 'friend' with two thumbs up, a London bus-stop sign complete with the word 'Wankers' and a T-shirt with the green sticker Will wore on his first day at Rudge Park Comp. And where would your average *Inbetweeners'* fan be without a good dose of 'clunge'? If you look hard enough, there's plenty of it about, the most popular T-shirt being 'I Love Clunge', which is a play on the famous 'I Love NYC' logo.

Misfits

The Inbetweeners are definitely misfits within Rudge Park Comp. Other than the 'freaks' who joined the school with Will McKenzie, they're seen as some of the least cool kids of their year but they're not the only misfits to break out from E4.

Hit British show *Misfits* follows a group of young offenders left with supernatural powers after being caught up in an unusual electrical storm while on community service. Although the storyline may at first seem completely different to the school sitcom, *The Inbetweeners* and *Misfits* have a lot in common.

Both shows follow the journeys of teens that don't fit in and, while the Inbetweeners strive to be in with the popular kids, the Misfits struggle with their new identities. This can even be seen in the personalities of one of the main characters from each of the shows: as Misfit Simon turns invisible when being ignored, Inbetweener Simon also seems to have the same problem, although usually with the ladies.

The cast of *The Inbetweeners* recognised the success of *Misfits* when Blake Harrison revealed in an E4 web chat with fans that *Misfits* is his favourite show on the channel, with Simon Bird also agreeing.

Like *The Inbetweeners*, *Misfits* has received great reviews from critics and fans alike. It was recognised alongside the school-based comedy when both shows were among the nominees at the Royal Television Society Programme Awards in 2009.

Did you know?
The Inbetweeners isn't the only E4 show planning to make the move across the Atlantic. Following an interview between the show's creator Howard Overman and Jonathan Ross in November 2010, speculation began that an American version of *Misfits* is being planned.

Miss Timbs

Played by Amanda St John, Miss Timbs is an attractive teacher at Rudge Park Comprehensive who appears in the 'Xmas Party' episode. She turns up at the start of the episode when the lads ogle her from afar and then again when she enters the party. Neil is quoted as saying, 'Very fit, very fit indeed!' Near the end of the episode, Neil tries to pull Miss Timbs; however, Mr Gilbert drags him away. Actress Amanda St John has had bit parts in British TV from around 1999, including shows such as *The Bill*, *Emmerdale*, *Coronation Street*, *Holby City* and *Doctors*.

In The Inbetweeners movie, the lads go to Malia in Crete for their summer holiday.

Movie

In September 2009, writers of *The Inbetweeners* Damon Beesley and Iain Morris confirmed that a movie version of the hit show had been commissioned. The only details revealed at the time were that the film would follow the four guys, now eighteen years old, as they go on holiday to boozy Crete resort Malia.

Morris told *Digital Spy* before the movie had been funded that they decided on the lads' holiday theme because for an eighteen-year-old the first holiday you take with your mates is a massive moment in life. It wasn't long before it really took off because Film4 jumped on board the project to fund it, while Ben Palmer took charge in the director's chair.

There had been rumours of the film a long while before it was announced and the cast of the series had shown great interest in whether it was to kick off. However, when the news was finally announced, it was dogged with rumours of ruckuses in camp. It was widely reported at the time that actor Simon Bird (Will) had made demands about pay. The rumours were dismissed by Iain Morris on Twitter, telling a fan questioning the whole episode: '[I] wouldn't believe everything you read. You can see photos of the lovely Simon Bird when I was with him yesterday.'

Thankfully, this didn't halt production and the journey of *The Inbetweeners* could be continued. Beesley then told the *Sun* that the movie 'is obviously an important part of the story. And then they are going to disappear and go off to different universities.' He said it would be hard for them to follow the characters at uni: 'It's very unlikely Neil is going to go!'

When *The Inbetweeners* first started, co-starring in a comedy was new to all four of the lead characters and it was no change with the movie. Joe Thomas (Simon) told the *Telegraph*: 'I don't think any of us are under the illusion that we're proper film stars.' Despite this, he was more than willing to put in the work before filming began. Actors are often called upon by film-makers to prepare for movie roles: this can mean getting into shape, or even *out* of shape, having a change of image or researching real-life characters, but for Joe, in usual *Inbetweeners'* fashion, the requirements for him were a bit more unusual.

Joe told the *Sun* that in preparation for the movie he had to take diving lessons for the scene where Joe's character dives off the boat: 'I want to make sure I can do it properly – I don't want to get injured.' In the end, he was coached by a former international diver who also taught actor Jason Statham. At least getting into something skimpy wasn't a problem, as Blake Harrison (Neil) revealed to *Digital Spy* that, for more than half the film, Joe would go to the dressing room for his costume only to find just a pair of pants! Hopefully, he didn't have the luck of his character Simon and this time everything stayed inside his 'budgie smugglers' – unlike at the fashion show!

The movie was actually filmed in Malia, Crete (where it is set), and Magaluf, Majorca – another popular destination with boozy British holidaymakers. The locations may not be the most glamorous of destinations, however: when Joe Thomas provided an online interview for ITV's *Daybreak*, he described Malia as 'a resort where British teenagers go to be sick'.

Even with his admission about the standards of the filming locations, this didn't stop the gang from having a good time. Joe told the *Sun* that, at the start of filming, it felt more like they were on holiday than actually at work. He said filming didn't begin until a few days into the stay so beforehand they were arranging trips out and lapping up the sun. He did admit that, once filming actually took off, the work did start to pile up and they realised they weren't on holiday, after all: 'Reality hit home by week three or four when we did some overnight shoots. That's when we realised that, although we were beside bars, we weren't ever going to go in.' But he says that, although there was plenty of hard work involved, they did have a lot of fun and were always in and out of each other's rooms and even organised a games night.

Gordon Smart from the *Sun* spotted James Buckley (Jay) while on location for *The Inbetweeners'* movie and tweeted: 'Just bumped into James Buckley in his tracksuit, playing pool with his girlfriend in Palmanova. That's the lifestyle I dream of…Cerveza!'

Fans could follow the fun the gang were having during filming through Blake Harrison's and writer Iain Morris's regular updates on their Twitter pages, which give a great insight into the making of the movie. From some of the tweets we've picked out, it looks as if they had a right laugh!

IAINKEVANMORRIS
JOE THOMAS HAS VERTIGO, BLAKE IS SCARED OF
FAST MOVING ZOMBIES, BUCKLEY IS SCARED OF
HARD WORK AND BIRD IS MADE OF ICE.

AFTER THREE SERIES AND A FILM, THE BOYS
CLUBBED TOGETHER AND GOT ME THESE
AMAZING GIFTS. THANKS GUYS: A SPERM
SHAPED VODKA SHOT, AND SOME SPANISH
BOOZE.

HAMMERED IN PALMA, WATCHING JOE TRYING TO
FLIP BEERMATS WHILST BLAKE TALKS ACTING. I
LOVE THEM. I AM ALSO DRUNK, I MAY HAVE
MENTIONED.

ALL THE GIRLFRIENDS ARE IN TOWN TONIGHT,
SO ME AND JOE THOMAS ARE STAYING AT A
HOTEL TOGETHER. NOT ENTIRELY SURE WHY.

BLAKEHARRISON23
FIRST PROPERLY WARM DAY WE'VE HAD IN
MALLORCA. BEATS FREEZING OUR ARSES OFF
AROUND NORTH LONDON PRETENDING IT'S JUNE
A LA' SERIES 2!

AFTER OVER 3 WEEKS AWAY I'M STARTING TO
GET NANDO'S WITHDRAWAL SYMPTOMS....I JUST
WANT A MEDIUM HALF CHICKEN!

FILMING DONE! IT'S SAD BUT NO TIME TO
WALLOW AS DRINKING IS AFOOT! THIS WAY TO
THE FINEST TANKARDS OF ALE MAGALUF HAS
TO OFFER!

As part of the fun the guys had on set, Blake Harrison admitted to the *Daily Star* that, during filming in Magaluf, he got stitched up by the cast. He wanted to make the effort to fit into the Spanish culture and so decided to learn some words and phrases to help him out. Joe Thomas and James Buckley saw this as a great opportunity to play a practical joke so the pair told him that the Spanish word '*culo*' meant 'cool'. It actually means 'arsehole' and so, while Blake was under the impression that he was making the effort with the Spanish, in reality he was insulting them – it's a moment where the actor seems to have taken on a resemblance to his onscreen character Neil!

As well as being the big-screen debut for the four main characters, the movie also introduces a gang of ladies played by Jessica Knappett (Lisa), Laura Haddock (Alison), Lydia Rose Bewley (Jane) and Tamla Kari (Lucy).

Jessica Knappett plays the role of Lisa, Neil's love interest, in *The Inbetweeners*' movie. Previously, she has appeared in the BBC sitcom *How Not To Live Your Life*, as has fellow *Inbetweeners*' movie actress Laura Haddock (Alison). Jessica has also made appearances in E4's *Meet the Parents* and BBC3's *Ideal*. In addition to acting, Jessica has also had success as a comedy writer and performer, particularly as a founder member of the sketch group *Lady Garden*. The six-member team has performed shows at The Comedy Store, The Gilded Balloon, The Hackney Empire and the Edinburgh Festival.

Laura Haddock plays Alison, Will's object of desire in the movie. She is best known for her role as Samantha in the BBC3 comedy *How Not To Live Your Life*. In this popular show, she plays the housemate to main character (Don) in the second series. A student, the character bears many resemblances to Don – unhappy with her job, bad relationship history and a keen drinker... sounds like an Inbetweener already!

Lydia Rose Bewley takes on the role of Jay's girl (Jane) in the movie. A newcomer to the screen, she has several theatre credits to her name including many performances as part of her education at The Oxford School of Drama. In the additional skills section of Lydia's Casting Call profile, it lists that she is good with children, having taught at a school, and it's probably the best attribute any actress could have working with the immature Inbetweeners!

Tamla Kari is another fresh face as she plays Simon's latest obsession Lucy in the movie. Another newcomer to the screen, Tamla also has significant theatre work behind her, thanks to her studies at the Drama Centre London.

The use of such new actresses in these roles might be seen by some to be a risk but the four *Inbetweeners'* leads

ACTRESS LAURA HADDOCK PLAYS ONE OF THE LOVELY LADIES TO BE ENCOUNTERED BY THE BOYS IN THE MOVIE.

were hired in similar circumstances and so it's no surprise that the writers and production team decided to go down this route.

Music

The music used in *The Inbetweeners* often sums up the sounds listened to by many of your average in-between teenagers living in suburban areas and cities around the UK. Most of the tracks used in the series are very much of-the-moment tunes, with the same style of indie rock, UK hip-hop and the occasional dance tune all the way through the three seasons. The theme tune – 'Gone Up in Flames' – is by Morning Runner.

Series One is dominated by the sounds of 'Foundations' (Kate Nash), 'Fluorescent Adolescent' (The Arctic Monkeys) and 'Kill the Director' (The Wombats) with a touch of Fratellis and Libertines thrown in for good measure, among many others. A lot of the best music in the first series comes in the 'Thorpe Park' episode when such artists as Jack Penate, Razorlight, Mark Ronson, Jamie T and The Chemical Brothers can all be heard. The 'Caravan Club' episode caters for a broader audience with songs from artists such as Justin Timberlake, Rihanna, Sugababes and George Michael all blasting out during the disco.

Series Two moves into a more distinct sound but

sticks to the alternative theme, with bands such as Razorlight, Mystery Jets, Vampire Weekend and The Cribs. Dido sums up the scene in Episode Three at Will's dinner party, and at the London club there are more chart-friendly tunes such as Eric Prydz and Dizzee Rascal. A couple of classic hits close Episodes Five and Six: The Cure's 'Just like Heaven' and The Jam's 'That's Entertainment', respectively.

Jamie T's 'Sticks and Stones' provides the background music to many of the scenes in Series Three. Most of the featured artists in the final series continue the trend from the previous two, with bands such as Marina & the Diamonds, Plan B, Pete And the Pirates, One Night Only and The Magic Numbers. Last, but by no means least, who could forget Lady Marmalade playing during Simon's fashion show balls-up?

During the airing of the third series of *The Inbetweeners*, all four lead characters appeared on the cover of the famous *NME* magazine. Normally reserved for bands and music icons, the foursome took to the cover as their alter egos in the show. Published on 13 October 2010, the edition also featured pictures of the lads causing chaos in the *NME* office.

Meanwhile, Mike Skinner was asked to produce the soundtrack for *The Inbetweeners*' movie in summer 2011. The Streets' hip-hop artist was said to be thrilled, being a big fan of the series. In 2011, Skinner announced that he would be retire from The Streets in order to pursue other ventures. The English–born rapper and producer is most famous for producing five hit albums with The Streets since 2000, including the critically acclaimed *Original Pirate Material* and *A Grand Don't Come For Free*. It is claimed that The Streets' hit single 'Fit But You Know It' was based around a lads' holiday, making Skinner the ideal person to produce the songs for *The Inbetweeners*' trip to Malia.

n is for...

Neil Sutherland

REPORT CARD

PE: F – Even when he remembers his kit, Neil is a poor student in this class. He needs to understand that running a few laps and playing football computer games does not qualify as revision.

Design and Technology: F – Neil fails to show any promise in Design and Technology. The only piece of work he has ever completed is a shelf that he claimed to have hung at his father's house.

Biology: F – Neil seems to be more interested in the movements of teacher Miss Timbs rather than the content of the lesson, although he has shown some promise during human reproduction lessons.

DOPEY NEIL SUTHERLAND
IS PLAYED BY BLAKE
HARRISON.

Contemporary Dance: A+ – An area where Neil has shown real promise. His excellent body popping has wowed teachers and pupils.

English: F – Having failed to learn any new skills on his work placement as a journalist, Neil continues to underachieve in this area.

Neil isn't the brightest bulb in the box, but he's a great Inbetweener. He gets a lot of stick from the others for his idiocy, as well as his gay dad, his mum running off and leaving them, his fit sister and general lack of money – and, because of this, he's responsible for some of the best bits on the show.

Neil has been mates with Jay and Si for years and, when Will comes along, there isn't much change as he's too clueless to even care. Despite this general lack of nous, Neil does come up with some belters throughout the series, often managing to shock the others.

In Series One, he reveals to the other Inbetweeners that he can actually drive, much to their disbelief. Asked why he didn't tell anyone sooner, he just says, 'You didn't ask.' So clueless is Neil that he bumbles along in life almost unaware of what he's doing, never mind the people around him.

Often he's the only one of the Inbetweeners to fall for Jay's bullshit stories about his sexploits but, on many occasions, it's Neil's own luck with the ladies that surprises us most. Throughout the series, he has numerous seen and unseen conquests, including Charlotte Hinchcliffe after she rejects Will, Big Kerry (after Will rejects her) and the punk girl at Caravan Club after she rejects Will! Do you see a pattern emerging here? Neil is great at swooping in after Will to steal the various loves of his life.

Maybe it's the fact that, out of all the Inbetweeners, Neil and Will are most different. While Will loves nothing more than trying to impress teachers, chairing events and generally being a geek, Neil takes a different approach. During exam season at Rudge Park Comp, while Will is revising, Neil decides to go for a run and play Pro Evolution Soccer – in preparation for his PE exams!

Neil is also the only one of the Inbetweeners to work. He's had two stints at ASDA and the comedy Mr Monkey job at Thorpe Park in the middle so really he's actually the most mature member of the group – a figurehead the others aspire to. After all, he's had sex, he works, he does OK with the ladies and he can drive. If only he wasn't such an idiot!

He's the first of the boys to lose his virginity (if you don't believe Jay and his 'many' conquests), but his first time wasn't so romantic as some may hope. After admiring his biology teacher Miss Timbs for so many years and eventually declaring his love for her, Neil definitely has a liking for older women. Having been seduced by an older lady at work (saucy ASDA Karen) on the cheese counter, at first Neil thinks he's going to be a father until he finds out that it wasn't a baby that she had… it was Chlamydia!

Strangely, this doesn't put him off and, delighted with his STI, Neil again manages to capture a more mature woman in the movie. Unfortunately, it's not the MILF of his dreams (Will's mum) but instead his former dinner lady! It seems Neil is more aroused by the smell of cheese and chip fat than a fragrant perfume.

FUNNIEST SCENE

Having admired his biology teacher Miss Timbs from afar, Neil decides that the Xmas Prom is his perfect opportunity to take their 'relationship' to the next level. So, after a session of body popping, he declares his love for Miss Timbs, leering all over her and trying to kiss her in front of everyone at the school: this is closely followed by a boner in his tight one-piece suit.

LOVES

Body popping and doing the robot
Miss Timbs, his biology teacher
Pro Evo Soccer

HATES

People calling his dad 'gay'
Bees in his Mr Monkey Suit
Exam revision

HOBBIES

At evenings and weekends, Neil can often be found upstairs putting small toy building bricks up his bum. He is also a keen dancer and has been known to body pop at several events.

Did you know?

In one of the deleted scenes of Series Three, it was revealed that Neil's middle name is Lindsay! Who knows why this didn't make the final cut? Maybe the writers thought he had enough stick from the others as it is!

The writers also admit that they wish they'd used jokes about Neil's mum running off more often. Normally, the boys concentrate on taking the piss out of his sister and his gay dad, but, in the final episode of Series Three, Jay brings his mum up in a tirade of insults: 'bent old man, wants to fuck his sister, mum did a legger!'

O is for...

Old People's Home ('The Duke of Edinburgh Awards': Series Two, Episode Five)

The infamous 'Duke of Edinburgh Awards' episode is the fifth in the second series, in which the foursome end up working at an old people's home, thanks to Will coordinating the sixth-form Duke of Edinburgh Award Scheme. After being given the honour by Mr Gilbert, he is promptly told to get out of his office.

Will's excitement is somewhat dampened by the other Inbetweeners when he arrives in the common room to deliver the news. Unfortunately for him, it's far more realistic than 'the school giving out free briefcases to specky twats' or 'Will's mum giving out free blowjobs' or even his make-believe appearance on 'Who's the gayest?' When he finally manages to deliver the good news, it's not met with the same enthusiasm. In order to rally the troops, Will tries to get the juices flowing but it seems Neil is still very confused: 'Who is this Duke of Edinburgh, is it King Philip?' After being told he wasn't, in fact, the King, Neil replies with the some typical logic: 'He fucks the Queen, though?' With that, they all decide to sign up, mostly due to the fact that there's nothing else going on in their lives.

The weekend rolls by and Will's mum is hosting a barbecue. While trying to keep the other three Inbetweeners in check (i.e. stopping them from going indoors and stealing his mum's knickers!), Will bumps into Daisy (the girl who used to babysit him as a child). Daisy is a university student who is working part-time at the local old people's home. For some reason, she seems to take a liking to Will and his 'funny walk', so this is the perfect opportunity for him to register an interest in voluntary work at the home… and maybe get lucky with an older, sophisticated woman at the same time.

Delivering the news to the others, Jay can't hide his delight and quickly announces that Will can't wait for a 'gum job' and that he definitely needs a 'queering aid'.

With those well-informed tidbits, the end of school arrives and it's time for their first shift at the home. Less than two minutes after being there, one of the residents confides in Will: 'Hello, I think I've done a poo!' Trying to sort out that mess, the inexperienced Will has to rely on Daisy's help. She duly obliges and Will makes sure he repays the favour by covering one of her shifts while she attends a hen night. Not only does Daisy agree for the four half-wits to cover her shift, she also agrees to go out to dinner with Will: the plan is coming together.

The next evening shift comes round and Neil and Jay are taking care of things. For Jay, the boredom is unbearable and inexplicably he decides to go for a quick tug. Strangely, Neil sets about helping him find somewhere to go: 'There's a bedroom down the hall they cleared out this morning, but they cleared it out because someone died in it – what if it's haunted?' The response from Jay leaves nothing to the imagination: 'Haunted or not, it'll be covered in ectoplasm when I've finished!' And off he goes…

After the night shift when Will covers for Daisy to get a date, Neil and Jay find Will asleep in the common room. Boys being boys, they decide that a little hair-removal cream is in order while Will catches up on forty winks, and so they proceed to squirt the tube inside his pants for a laugh. When the day is over and the cream has done its business, Will confides in Simon:

his only explanation is that he has 'spunked his pants in the common room' and then all of his pubes have fallen out! Understandably, Simon can't figure out what's gone on, but still attempts to offer some advice such as drawing some pubes on with a marker pen or wearing a cock wig! This advice is not well received and just makes Will more irate: 'Good idea, after that maybe I draw a six-pack on my stomach or a longer cock!'

Despite Simon's terrible advice, it's time for the date and, as Will goes to pick Daisy up from the old people's home, he spots an old man's wig. Suddenly, Simon's advice isn't looking so bad after all. Following a rush of blood to the head, he takes the wig and stuffs it down his pants.

The date looks to be going extremely well for Will, which is surprising, considering he has a cock wig down his pants! At the end of it, he even gets a kiss from Daisy and, what's more, an invite back to her house – which has nothing to do with the bottle of wine she had at dinner! Even so, his plan to bed his ex-babysitter is working, or at least it is until she pulls the cock wig out of his pants while frolicking on the bed. 'What the fuck is this?' is the natural response of any person in that situation and, after Will confesses that he doesn't actually have any hair down there, Daisy thinks it best to stop as she thinks he is too young to be getting up to such antics. Naturally, Will disagrees. 'Forget about the hair, it still works! Just touch it, you might like it,' he pleads with her.

Meanwhile, there's still voluntary work to be done and, as the others continue their work at the home, Jay searches for new material for his latest wanking crusade (sadly, he has already worn out the pictures in most of the magazines lying around, including Fern Britton in *Hello!* magazine). So, as usual, Jay finds what he thinks is a quiet, empty room to do the deed. Luckily, there's a picture of a scantily clad woman in there, albeit from the 1960s but that's enough for him. As he reaches his climax, a light is switched on and an old woman is lying peacefully in bed: 'Don't worry, love, I've seen it all before' is her strangely calm comment.

Could anything be worse than wanking in a room with an old woman over a picture of herself when she was younger? Well, yes, as that same old woman's son walks into the room with Daisy. As the man takes Jay's hand to shake it as a thank you for all his hard work, he gets a palm full of spunk! 'He did that looking at me,' says the old lady, extremely proud.

Thanks to Jay, the lads are thrown off the Duke of Edinburgh scheme and Will fails to land an older woman. Added to that, they have to deal with the wrath of Mr Gilbert.

Did you know?
The old lady's son is played by Christopher Young, who has also produced all eighteen episodes of *The Inbetweeners*. His brief cameo at the end of the programme is his only appearance in the hit show.

P is for...

Pamela Cooper

BACKGROUND

Pamela is the playful mum of Inbetweener Simon. Although she sometimes plays the mumsy role, such as keeping an open-door policy on her son when he has girls round the house and giving him a stern telling-off every now and then, she has a more sizzling side.

Pamela can often be found in romantic embraces with her husband Alan, much to Si's displeasure. The pair can always be seen canoodling around the house, making no attempt to hide their attraction from their

Actress Robin Weaver plays Simon's mum, Pamela.

sons, although Simon seems to take far more offence than his younger brother Andrew.

Although Pamela is obviously madly in love with Alan, he's not the only man to seize her attention in the series. When she invites her French friend's son (Patrice) over to stay, like most women, she takes an immediate liking to him, much to Simon's disgust. But Alan doesn't mind the attention Pamela gives the younger man, admitting he hasn't got youth on his side, although he can more than make up for it with experience (or so he says!).

FUNNIEST SCENE

Pamela's most amusing scene involves her husband Alan, Will, Simon, Polly McKenzie and Kevin Sutherland. When Will and Simon's parents catch the boys bunking off from school, they start to give them a stern telling-off. To get out of trouble, Simon decides to accuse Neil's dad of 'touching' them and Will goes down the route of admitting to having an alcohol problem. However, Pamela and the other parents don't fall for these terrible lies and instead burst out laughing.

LOVES

Simon, when he passes his driving test

HATES

When Simon lies about bunking off
The smell of Simon's hair gel

> *Did you know?*
> Actress Robin Weaver was over eight months pregnant when the final episode of Series Three was filmed. If you pay attention, you will notice that the camera only shows her upper body to hide the bump.

Patrice

Played by French actor Vladimir Consigny, Patrice is an exchange student who stays at Simon's house to help him to become a more confident French speaker. He is renowned for his good looks and charm with the ladies, but also for being slightly racist. Patrice appears in the 'Will's Birthday' episode and in the space of one day he urinates in a garden, pulls Charlotte 'Big Jugs' Hinchcliffe and makes a rude comment to some underage girls in the street. During his stay, he bumps into Will's mum, who instantly takes a liking to him (and vice versa), so much so that Patrice tells Will that he has just 'masturbated over her' later in the episode. In addition to appearing in *The Inbetweeners*, Vladimir has appeared in well-known French films *Hellphone* and *Wild Grass*.

Did you know?
During filming, Vladimir Consigny made the crew stop the car en route to a location so that he could urinate in the middle of a street. Talk about getting into character!

Peep Show

The longest-running sitcom in Channel 4's history, *Peep Show* has enjoyed seven seasons and is still going

INBETWEENERS WRITER IAIN MORRIS WAS A SCRIPT EDITOR ON PEEP SHOW STARRING DAVID MITCHELL AND ROBERT WEBB.

strong today. It stars the British comedians David Mitchell and Robert Webb. Mitchell and Webb met with the writers of *The Inbetweeners*, Iain Morris and Damon Beesley, when working on *The 11 O'Clock Show* in the late 1990s. Morris then went on to become script editor of *Peep Show* until 2004 before leaving to set up Bwark Productions with his writing partner, Damon Beesley.

Peep Show follows the journey of two men, Mark and Jeremy, who have two completely different personalities and outlooks on life. The show received critical acclaim and admiration due to its style of 'point of view' camera angles. *Peep Show* has claimed many awards during its time on air, most notably Best Situation Comedy at the 2008 BAFTAs.

Polly McKenzie (Will's Fit Mum)

Will's attractive mum is often described as 'the MILF' by Neil, Simon and Jay. After splitting up with her husband who moved away, Mrs McKenzie moves Will from a posh private school where briefcases and blazers are the norm to a state comprehensive, where bullying and bravado go hand in hand.

After picking up Will from his first day at the new school, Will's mum almost grants him entry into the circle of trust within his three new friends simply because of how fit she is. Mrs McKenzie often tries to shelter Will from the dangers of girls, d.r.u.g.s. and the threat of not wearing a sweater on a chilly day. What's more, she will sometimes knock his confidence by calling him 'sensible' in the patronising manner that only mothers can get away with. Similarly, Will is very protective of his mother, in particular when he is left home alone in Episode Five of Series Three. Polly goes off on a weekend away with Fergus, a man whom she went to college with and, following her divorce, was reunited with via the social networking site Facebook.

Polly McKenzie is played by English actress Belinda Stewart-Wilson (born in 1971). Her acting career has been a healthy mix, from drama to sitcoms and impersonation-based comedy shows. In the mid-1990s, she appeared in famous British TV shows such as Agatha Christie's *Poirot* and *Goodnight Sweetheart*. After several appearances throughout the years in the likes of *Holby City* and *Starting Out*, she began to forge her way into the comedy scene, starting in 2005 with the BBC Worldwide comedy spoof *Broken News* – a satirical look at current affairs worldwide. Following this, she made a brief appearance in *Bremner, Bird and Fortune*, then multiple appearances in *The Peter Serafinowicz Show*, *The IT Crowd* and of course as Polly McKenzie in *The Inbetweeners*. After the popular E4 series, she was in high demand and was soon working on BBC projects such as *The Armstrong*

& *Miller Show*, *Miranda* and *The Impressions Show*, where she impersonated Nigella Lawson.

In 2011, along with appearing in *The Inbetweeners'* film, Belinda also made an appearance in *FHM* magazine's 100 Sexiest Women of 2011, the tag of 'MILF' in the long-running series almost certainly helping her case.

Belinda has a four-year-old son with Ben Miller of *Armstrong & Miller Show* fame; however, it is believed the couple are now separated. They played alongside each other in his comedy sketch show and the TV series *Primeval*.

Production Company

The production company behind *The Inbetweeners* is Bwark Productions, which was founded in 2004 by the writers Damon Beesley and Iain Morris. The pair decided to set up their own company following years of experience in writing comedy and working for Channel 4 in various roles. Based in London, Bwark have produced some of Britain's funniest TV shows. Aside from *The Inbetweeners*, they have produced various Jimmy Carr stand-up DVDs as well as the acclaimed Channel 4 comedy series *Free Agents*.

In 2007, Bwark produced a pilot show – *The Scum Also Rises* – commissioned by BBC3, which later went

'WILL'S FIT MUM', POLLY, IS PLAYED BY BELINDA STEWART-WILSON.

on to be called *The Persuasionists* after securing a six-part series on BBC2. The sitcom revolved around a group of people who work in a fictional advertising agency (HHH&H) and starred Iain Lee (known to Beesley and Morris from *The 11 O'Clock Show*), Simon Farnaby (*The Mighty Boosh*) and Adam Buxton of *Adam & Joe* fame. Also, in 2007 Channel 5 commissioned *Angelo's*, a six-part series to be produced by Bwark. This was a sitcom based around characters working in a central London greasy-spoon cafe and starred comedians such as Steve Brody and Miranda Hart.

Before the filming of the 2011 *Inbetweeners'* movie, Bwark Productions denied reports of a pay rift between themselves and Simon Bird, who plays Will McKenzie. It was reported that Bird had been demanding more money before shooting the movie and the production team were unwilling to buckle to his demands. Reports claimed he was making such demands due to his added input into the show as the main character and also as the narrator – Will McKenzie appears more than any other character. Executive producer and writer of the show Iain Morris denied reports of a rift between both parties and went on to quash the rumours on Twitter.

For *The Inbetweeners'* film, Bwark Productions worked in association with Young Films, a company run by Christopher Young, one of the producers of *The Inbetweeners*. Young Films have produced a collection of low-key movies, which have won awards at numerous domestic and international film festivals.

In 2011, Bwark Productions donated £500 to Comic Relief for every 'rude location' found on *The Inbetweeners*' Rude Road Trip (*see also* Rude Road Trip). In the end, the lads found 52 rude place names!

q is for...

Qualified Drivers

For all the Inbetweeners, driving comes high on the priority list, although some have more luck than others. For Simon, Jay, Neil and Will, driving represents the opportunity to gain freedom from parents and to try their chances with the opposite sex. As Will explains, 'Boys who drive are a whole lot more attractive than those who don't!'

Being the oldest, Simon is the first of the group to begin his driving lessons. Quite literally, they go off with a bang as in Series One, Episode Three, 'Thorpe Park', while on a driving lesson he reverses into another car as he practises parallel parking. His instructor panics and makes him drive off – not the start Simon had hoped for!

His luck then goes from bad to worse on the day of the big test. Simon struggles to pass the basic eye test before even getting into the car, which he then stalls on his first attempt at driving out of the test centre. There's only one thing that gets him through his driving test successfully, though: the examiner. When Simon stalls the car, she appears to have taken a liking to him and tells him not to worry, that she can help (as she squeezes his thighs!). As they drive out of the test centre, she instructs him just to steer and says that she will work the pedals. We never find out what happens to Simon on his driving test, but he passes and, given the advances of his examiner, it's doubtful that it was due to his road awareness!

Series Two starts off with Jay now in the driving seat. It's assumed that he has passed his test during the summer holidays, but it's revealed in Series Three that he's been driving on his provisional licence! On the first day of the new term, he picks the lads up for school in his 'Minge Mobile'. Will points out that the name he has given the vehicle probably isn't the best thing to call your mum's car, but Jay doesn't care. All he can think about is the pulling power the car will give him. In fact, Jay's driving is so bad that Will likens himself to Lady Di – with risk of death imminent. Before Jay can start 'pulling the birds', he first needs to figure out how roundabouts work!

In the first series, Neil reveals he too can drive and tells the guys how he has a new car that he's been doing up. When the others see the suped-up car they're very impressed: nice paintjob, good rims, even stickers on the back window… It's a real chav mobile, but it's just what the lads want to attract some female attention and to avoid having to get into Si's yellow box on wheels.

There's just one problem with Neil's car, however – it has no engine! The lads find out after Neil offers to drive them all to London. When they turn up at his house and lust over the car, he breaks the news. It's another Inbetweeners' moment where they all wonder why on earth Neil didn't make the revelation earlier. What an idiot! The car isn't seen again through the series – you can only assume he never did manage to get an engine for it.

But Neil does have an engine in the moped he's given for his birthday and this time it looks like the real deal. Although the lads won't all be able to bunk lifts, Neil will have some cred on the new bike. There's only one problem: his good friend Jay. Before Neil has even got the bike off the forecourt, Jay manages to crash the thing. He decides he's qualified to drive the bike first because his dad was mates with Lance Armstrong (yes, *the* cyclist!), but, heading straight into the wall, he completely writes off Neil's gift. Again, as with the car, you don't see the bike again after this incident. Poor Neil – he comes so close to twice getting wheels, but falls at the final hurdle!

Driving is important to Will, too. Maybe it would have been the final piece of the puzzle in impressing Charlotte 'Big Jugs' Hinchcliffe, but thanks to his

THE CAR'S THE STAR.

parents' divorce Will gets a vest for his seventeenth birthday instead of the set of keys he'd hoped for. Now he must jump lifts in two of the worst vehicles in history: Simon's and Jay's mum's cars.

In the movie, all four of the Inbetweeners finally get their own wheels. Four wheels and room for a passenger, it must be a car? No, instead they hire quad bikes and take them down the Malia club strip in classic 'Brits abroad' fashion!

Did you know?
James Buckley (Jay) said he loved doing the driving scene – 'it just made the day so much fun' – with Simon Bird (Will) and Blake Harrison (Neil) voting James the better driver over Joe Thomas (Simon). With so much time spent shooting in the cars, Simon and Blake were often back passengers and in healthy positions to judge the skills of both drivers.

r is for...

Rachel

Carli's friend Rachel appears in the 'Night Out in London' episode in Series Two. After Will gets wind that Rachel may be interested in him, things start to go terribly wrong in the queue for the club when she asks: 'Is it OK if I stand with my back to you? I just don't want people to think I'm with you!' After Will tries to pull her again in the club, she takes her interest elsewhere. Rachel appears on two other occasions after this: once, at the end of Series Two when Carli asks Simon if she can go to his house to revise, and again at the end of Series Three in the canteen, when Carli tells Simon she has heard the news about him moving away. The part is played by actress

Lily Lovett, who before appearing in *The Inbetweeners* featured in the TV shows *Doctors* and *Coming Up*.

Ricky Gervais

Co-writers of the show Iain Morris and Damon Beesley met Ricky Gervais while working on the late-night Channel 4 programme *The 11 O'Clock Show*. Gervais and his writing partner Stephen Merchant have written some of Britain's most groundbreaking and best-loved comedy shows, most notably *The Office* and *Extras*. In the second series of *Extras*, they even named two characters after Iain and Damon.

In 2003, it is rumoured that Ricky injured his back while wrestling with Iain Morris. Apparently, there is

IAIN MORRIS AND DAMON BEESLEY WORKED WITH RICKY GERVAIS ON THE 11 O'CLOCK SHOW.

video footage of the incident, although this has never been broadcast. Gervais subsequently mentioned the accident during his XFM radio show and has also talked about his back problems every now and again during his stand-up career.

Roy

Will's neighbour and a fellow tank-top enthusiast is Roy. He appears in Episode Five of Series Two, the Duke of Edinburgh Awards' saga. When Will's mum hosts a barbecue at her house, there is a scene when Roy is chatting to Will and asks him if he should be revising, after Will explains that he is having a day off. Roy then tells him an awkward tale: 'My nephew went to Centre Parks six weeks before his entrance exam to Oxford: he didn't make the cut and decided to take a year out. All his friends went to university – by the time they'd returned for Christmas, he hanged himself.' Will thanks Roy for his advice and quickly moves on to talk to someone else.

The character of Roy is played by the veteran actor Colin Spaull, whose acting credits go way back to the 1950s when he played major roles as a child actor in TV shows. Through his later years, he took on parts in classic British TV shows such as *Z Cars* and *Dixon of Dock Green*. More recently, he has had recurring roles in *The Bill*, *Doctor Who* and *Holby City*.

Rude Road Trip

In aid of Comic Relief 2011, the four Inbetweeners embarked on a 'Rude Road Trip', visiting some of the rudest and crudest place names across the UK. The challenge was to visit 50 of the filthiest place names in

BUSH
LANE EC4

LE·ON

The lads and Greg Davies
(Mr Gilbert) find a location
on the Rude Road Trip.

just 50 hours. Obviously, any Inbetweeners' road trip wouldn't be the same without the Fiat Cinquecento Hawaii (red door included).

For the road trip, the gang were filmed non-stop, inside and out of the car as they crossed the country in their search. They were sponsored £500 for every location they visited, with Greg Davies (Mr Gilbert) launching the challenge on Tuesday, 18 January. As part of the 50 filthy names the guys needed to find, Davies included personal challenges for the four. These were 'Bell End' for Simon Bird (Will), 'Twatley' for Blake Harrison (Neil), 'Titty Ho' for James Buckley (Jay) and, to add a spanner in the works, 'Quim' for Joe Thomas (Simon). Joe's personal challenge was harder than any other to complete because 'Quim' doesn't exist as a place name. This was actually added by Davies to spice up the challenge of the road trip – something the other three knew all about.

Day One of the 50-hour adventure starts at 'Bush Lane' and then it's on to 'Pump Alley'. Guided by the aptly named 'Twat Nav', the first day also takes the guys to 'Fanny's Lane', 'Swallow Drive', for a bite to eat at 'Sally Pussey's Inn' and 'Twatley' – with Blake the first to complete his personal challenge.

Last stop of Day One of the challenge is 'Cock Street' in Newport, but when the four arrive they discover someone has already stolen the sign and, in a moment of creative genius, Blake (Neil) makes his own crudely crafted sign, even adding in the Welsh underneath!

Day Two begins with 27 hours and 17 minutes remaining of the 50-hour challenge but the gang are really up against it, having only managed 11 places on the first day despite driving from London to Wales!

Simon Bird is first to complete his personal challenge on Day Two of the fundraiser: at 'Bell End'. Next on the list is 'Hawes Lane' (whore's), with James asking, 'Doesn't your mum live on here, Joe?'

As Joe's hunt for the elusive 'Quim' continues, he starts harassing locals as to its whereabouts following a tip-off phone call to say that it's nearby. It's only then that Blake and Simon decide to let Joe in on the joke that he's searching for a place that doesn't exist. Despite them offering to add an extra tenner each to the Comic Relief pot, Joe replies, 'I feel soiled!'

At the end of Day Two in a hotel, the gang start to wonder whether they've bitten off more than they can chew, having visited 28 places so far with another 22 to get to on the final day in just 5 hours and 54 minutes.

Up against it, and back in London, the four decide to split up into pairs at their first destination ('Purves Road'). With Blake and James in the car and Simon and Joe on foot, they plan to meet back on Cock Lane at the end of the challenge with the hope of getting to the magic 50.

News comes in on the final stretch that a news agency

has offered to add an additional £500 per location found during the last three hours of the challenge! This puts even more pressure on the guys, but, thanks to 'Cumming Street', 'Bonar Road', 'Pratt Walk' and a few more, they manage to visit 52 locations.

Eventually, the boys raised over £50,000 for their efforts and a delighted Simon Bird admits they didn't realise the challenge they faced: 'We really underestimated how difficult this challenge was going to be. We didn't think we were going to make it, but we pulled it out of the bag on the day. Having completed the challenge, we feel on top of the world!'

When the Comic Relief Challenge ended, the actual Cinquecento to feature in all three series of *The Inbetweeners* was auctioned off. The clapped-out old banger proved a popular hit with fans of the show and sold for over £21,000 – even though its MOT had almost expired! Here's the eBay listing for the comedy motor:

THIS IS THE GENUINE ARTICLE! NOT ONLY THE ACTUAL CAR FEATURED IN THE HIT TV SHOW BUT IT'S THE VEHICLE RESPONSIBLE FOR GETTING THE FOUR BOYS TO SOME OF THE RUDEST PLACE NAMES IN THE UK.

SO BID NOW!!! YOU'LL IMPRESS YOUR FRIENDS WITH THIS UNIQUE MOTOR, COMIC RELIEF WILL SPEND ALL THE MONEY YOU BID ON LIFE-CHANGING PROJECTS, AND THE SUN WILL SHINE. (THAT LAST BIT ABOUT THE SUN MIGHT NOT BE TRUE.)

Did you know?

Here's a full list of all the filthy places visited by the Inbetweeners for Comic Relief:

1. Bush Lane, City of London
2. Pump Alley, Brentford
3. Beaver Close, Hampton
4. Cock-a-Dobby, Sandhurst
5. Fanny's Lane, Bucklebury
6. Old Sodom Lane, Chippenham

FILMING FOR THE RUDE ROAD TRIP

7. Sally Pussey's Inn, Swindon
8. Cock Street, Redwick
9. Twatley, Malmesbury
10. Bottoms Farm Lane, Doynton
11. Swallow Drive, Patchway
12. Minge Lane, Upton Upon Severn
13. North Piddle, Grafton Flydord
14. Licky End, Bromsgrove
15. Bell End, Rowley Regis
16. Hawes Lane, Sandwell
17. Winkle Street, Sandwell
18. Balls Street, Walsall
19. Balls Hill, Walsall
20. Willey, Lutterworth
21. The Cock Inn, Roade
22. Titty Ho, Raunds
23. Butts Road, Raunds
24. Weedon, Northamptonshire
25. Adams Bottom, Leighton-Linslade
26. Seamons Close, Dunstable
27. Snatchup, Redbourn
28. Ass House Lane, Bushey
29. Purves Road, Brent
30. Swallow Street, Westminster
31. Melon Place, Kensington
32. The Ring, Westminster

33. Hookers Road, Waltham Forest
34. Hoe Street, Walthamstow
35. Swallow Place, Westminster
36. Melon Road, Waltham Forest
37. Nelson's Column, Trafalgar Square
38. Ming Street, Tower Hamlets
39. Mudchute DLR Station, Poplar
40. Cumming Street, Islington
41. Cold Blow Lane, Lewisham
42. Bonar Road, Camberwell
43. Roger Street, Camden
44. Thrush Street, Southwark
45. Pratt Walk, Lambeth
46. Trump Street, London
47. Rood Lane, London
48. Staining Lane, London
49. Back Passage, London
50. Cock Hill, London
51. Helmet Row, Islington
52. Cock Lane, London

S is for...

Samantha

Played by actress and stand-up comedian Jo Maycock, Samantha is Jay's ideal girl. She is seen in the last episode of Series One with Carli in the canteen when she calls Simon 'sick boy boner' and at the end of the episode at the Xmas party. Samantha approaches Jay when he is talking to Big John at the burger counter and immediately it's clear she has similar characteristics to Jay, i.e. she is also a bullshitter as she tells Jay she can get him a gig as a DJ at one of Ibiza's top clubs. The pair seem to get on like a house on fire and, at the end of the party, Jay explains to the others how he got a blowjob behind the DJ booth when in fact, allegedly, it was only a hand-job. Before appearing in *The Inbetweeners*, Jo performed stand-up comedy at various events, and currently has her own YouTube channel with comedy workshops and stand-up tips.

Sex And The Chippy

Dubbed the female version of *The Inbetweeners* by *Broadcast*, *Sex And The Chippy* is one of E4's latest comedy outings. The series follows a group of women in their early thirties talking about nights out in a Liverpool chip shop.

Inbetweeners' director Ben Palmer was originally slated to direct the sitcom; however, he had to pass the director's chair on to the legendary British comedian Harry Enfield after commitments with *The Inbetweeners'* movie meant he was no longer able to work on the show.

The show's writers, Neil Jones and Heather Robson of *Hollyoaks*, told the *Liverpool Echo*: 'We pitched it as the older sisters of *The Inbetweeners* if they were from Liverpool. The women have boring jobs and go out every weekend to escape their routines and look for a bit of romance but every week it turns out to be disastrous and the episode starts at the end of the night with their chips.'

Channel 4's head of comedy Shane Allen recognises the similarities to *The Inbetweeners*, describing it as 'glossy, raucous, upbeat and entertaining', and added,

'We're delighted with the script. It's bursting with great banter and some truly jaw-dropping set pieces. It's so good to be getting behind something female, funny and young for E4 to complement *The Inbetweeners*.'

Maybe it's a good thing that the guys were out in Malia while this particular series was being filmed. We know Neil has a certain soft spot for the older lady – particularly if it involves food!

Simon Bird

The character Will in the show is played by the actor Simon Bird who is often seen as the lead because he narrates all three seasons. Simon was born on 19 August 1984 and, before starting out on his acting career, he studied English at Cambridge University. While at university, Simon began his fledgling acting career as the president of the Cambridge University Footlights Dramatic Club, more commonly known as Footlights – a theatrical club that has grown in stature for its comedy and stand-up performances. Other famous faces to have plied their trade at Footlights include Stephen Fry, David Baddiel, John Cleese and Bird's co-star in *The Inbetweeners* Joe Thomas (Simon).

Joe was to have an immediate effect on Bird's comedy career: after he finished a Masters at the University of London, the two set up a comedy sketch show together

SIMON BIRD PLAYS
WILL MACKENZIE.

and performed at the Edinburgh comedy festival in 2007 and 2008. Along with writing and performing in sketch shows, Bird has also tried his hand at stand-up comedy and performed for four years running at Chortles National Student Comedy Awards. Some would say the performances put Simon on the comedy radar and made him well known within the comedy circuit – and, most importantly, also to the writers of *The Inbetweeners*, Iain Morris and Damon Beesley.

In 2008, Morris and Beesley invited Bird to audition for the role of Will in *The Inbetweeners*. He got the part and would become the focal point for the show. After the first series in 2008, Bird won a British Comedy Award for Best Male Newcomer, and at the same ceremony in 2009 he won the Best Comedy Actor award.

After the third series of *The Inbetweeners*, Bird co-wrote and starred in a BBC3 comedy show entitled *The King is Dead*, along with co-presenters Nick Mohammed and Katy Wix. The show revolved around a panel involving Bird hypothetically interviewing celebrities to replace someone in a high position of authority such as 'The King', 'The Chief of Police' and 'The President of the USA'. In a series of rounds, the comedic panel would grill the celebrities to determine who would take the position at the end of the show. Among the celebs to appear on *The King is Dead* are James Corden, Caprice, Louis Walsh and Terry Nutkins.

SIMON COOPER, PLAYED BY JOE
THOMAS, IS THE PROUD OWNER
OF HIS 'BENDER MOBILE', THE
FIAT CINQUECENTO.

In 2011, Bird starred alongside Tamsin Greig and Tom Rosenthal in the comedy *Friday Night Dinner*, a series in which two brothers go to their parents' house for dinner every week as tradition. The sitcom is written by the award-winning writer and comedy performer Robert Popper, who, along with many British comedians, made his first comedy appearances on Channel 4's *The 11 O'Clock Show* and has worked on many of the channel's best programmes, including *Peep Show*, *Bo Selecta* and, of course, *The Inbetweeners*.

Did you know?
Tom Rosenthal, who plays Simon Bird's brother in *Friday Night Dinner*, is the son of TV sports presenter Jim Rosenthal.

Simon Cooper

REPORT CARD

Chemistry: C – Not much to speak of with girls, but marks for effort.

Fashion: F – Marked down severely for catwalk disaster.

Drama: A – Plenty of it when Simon is around!

Geography: D – Loss of marks for getting lost in London.

Business Studies: E – Simon paid £20 and a pair of new trainers for some tramp's shoes – must try harder!

BACKGROUND

Simon is the hopeless romantic with a typical teenage streak: having to find love and put up with his parents' up-and-down relationship is the hardest of tasks, not to mention a little brother back home to piss him off all the more. His constant fear of embarrassment and moody behaviour often lands him in more trouble than it's worth.

Simon's closest friend is Will, although they didn't get off to the best of starts when they met on the first day. Mr Gilbert tasked Simon with looking after the new kid whereupon he instantly initiated a verbal attack on the new boy: 'His shoes are clumpy and his hair's a bit gay!'

Along with taking the title of lovesick teenager, as the only one to drive in the early days, Simon also assumes the role of chauffeur, driving his three friends in the bright-yellow Special Edition Fiat Cinquecento Hawaii (otherwise known as the 'Bender Mobile') past bus stops to theme parks and to the famous Caravan Club.

FUNNIEST SCENE

When schoolmate Carli D'Amato (Emily Head) invites Simon round for an evening helping to babysit her little brother, Jay advises his friend to get drunk before he goes round to make him seem cooler: 'Right, whisky, vodka and load of crème de menthe – when she sees you after this, she'll be frothing at the gash!'

Will manages to wangle his way into Carli's house while Simon takes care of 'business'. Steaming drunk, Will decides to teach Carli's brother about nuclear terrorism and Simon begins his outrageous wooing of Carli by asking her to 'finger herself' in front of him.

At this point, Simon begins to feel a little queasy and throws up all over the kitchen worktop, down the sink and all over Carli's brother's face!

Did you know?
In order for this scene to be realistic, they had to use a 'vomit machine', a vacuum cleaner device

attached to Simon and filled with vegetable soup. The machine was strategically placed on his leg with a tube that ran up his body and out near his mouth.

LOVE INTERESTS

Simon is the one character in the series that you would say tries to be romantic but, unfortunately, he sometimes tries a little too hard. He always seems to have the best intentions, but they don't always go to plan: a couple of brief encounters at Caravan Club and some fondling at the school disco really don't count towards his longing for a lasting relationship.

Simon's lifelong love for family friend Carli D'Amato begins to develop sparks in the sixth-form common room when he catches a glimpse down her shirt and develops what is described by Jay as a 'stalk-on' and he quickly proceeds to announce it to the whole room.

The path to Carli's heart has inevitably been full of barriers, including Simon's complete inability to have a normal conversation and a certain lanky rugby-playing guy named Tom. One of the defining moments in their relationship nearly comes at the end of Series One when Simon teams up with Jay to stop the music in the middle of the school prom and declare his love. Fortunately, he is spared his blushes and interrupted by the sight of Neil desperately trying to seduce Miss

Timbs. However, in the last episode of Series Two, Simon and Carli share a kiss while revising for their end-of-year exams, but Simon's visit to Cloud 9 doesn't last too long before he is brought back down to earth at the end-of-year piss-up. As he passes her the mix-tape he has made for her, she announces that she is back with her ex-boyfriend Tom.

In Series Three, Carli is forgotten for a while as new girl Tara comes on the scene. She was to be Simon's first real girlfriend but after an eventful trip to Warwick she immediately called it off via text; therefore, the only natural thing is for Simon to start pining over Carli again. At the end of Series Three, things with Carli are left up in the air when she gets the news that Simon is moving away to Swansea. When he receives a text message from her near the end of the episode, his response is 'brilliant!', although the contents of the message are never revealed.

LOVES
Carli D'Amato
Tara
Driving

HATES
His little brother Andrew
Swansea
Lanky rugby players

HOBBIES

Simon loves strutting his stuff on the catwalk, although his 'unique' style has been criticised for being too revealing! He's also a big fan of road trips and often takes the other Inbetweeners on unforgettable adventures in his shitty yellow car.

SKINS IS ANOTHER HIT E4 TEEN SHOW. THE LADS FROM THE INBETWEENERS AGREE THAT WHILE SKINS IS THE TEEN FANTASY, THE INBETWEENERS IS MORE THE REALITY.

Skins

Hit E4 teen-drama *Skins* has been dubbed one of the coolest teenage dramas around, following the lives of a group of three generations of Bristolian teenagers through sixth form.

Simon Bird (Will) told the BBC that he thinks *The Inbetweeners* gives a more honest depiction of teenage life than *Skins*: '*Skins* is great because it's this fantasy of what you want your teenage years to be whereas *The Inbetweeners* is what your teenage years actually were.'

Co-star Joe Thomas (Simon) added, '*The Inbetweeners* is more the time you spend not having the night that you thought you were gonna be having. Waiting to get somewhere, waiting for a bus to take you to a village [where] you might get into somebody's house party, that's the territory that we're involved in.'

When *Digital Spy* asked James Buckley (Jay) if he thinks *The Inbetweeners* is the 'Anti-*Skins*', he told them that *Skins* represents the lifestyle a teenager would love to have: 'rolling into a party, pulling some amazing-looking girl and getting into trouble'. From the luck of *The Inbetweeners*, we know this certainly isn't the case: it's more climb over a fence to get into a party, get covered in shit, get bullied by Donovan and go home alone!

> *Did you know?*
> It's not just *The Inbetweeners* that has made a big impact stateside. MTV have ordered a remake of Skins. Its US premiere was January 2011, amid much controversy over its storylines of casual teenage sex and drug use of underage characters.

Sleeping Beauty

The Inbetweeners' version of *Sleeping Beauty* isn't quite like the fairytale you may have heard about. Instead of a story of a faraway land, princesses, wizardry and magic, it's actually a form of self-pleasure!

First introduced in Series Two, Episode Three 'Will's Birthday', Neil gives a graphic description of this 'technique': 'You sit on your arm till your hand goes dead. Ten to fifteen minutes is normally enough, and then, when you wank, it feels like someone else is doing it.'

Jay claims the 'Sleeping Beauty' was invented by his mate's brother saying he and his mates were known as the 'Dead-hand Gang'.

Later in the same episode, we see the 'Sleeping Beauty' put into practice in a hilarious scene in Jay's bedroom. There he is, laptop at the ready, saucy movie blaring away and hand dead when his mum and Neil walk into the room!

Screaming at the pair not to enter and in a fit of panic, he struggles with his limp hand trying to close the laptop down. He tries and tries, but after sitting on his arm for so long he just can't get it closed. Not what any mum would want to see, but a great comedy moment of the series!

Supporting Artists

Like many sitcoms, *The Inbetweeners* relies on the work of a crew of supporting actors to give its scenes credibility and realism.

During the filming of the first series, each of the Inbetweeners was given a camera to record a video diary of their experiences. Simon Bird (Will) and Blake Harrison (Neil) both reveal in their diaries that James Buckley (Jay) took a liking to one of the show's supporting artists.

In Simon Bird's diary, Buckley was probed over the incident, to which he responded that he didn't want to reveal her name because 'there's going to be a lot of supporting artists thinking I'm talking about them'. Of course he was joking, but it's good to see he doesn't follow his character's philosophy on women! The video diaries do reveal, however, that he did try it on with a few supporting artists. Blake told of his favourite moment on set when Buckley invented a party back at his hotel room after filming, just on the off-chance of trying to chat them up.

Susie

Played by Anabel Barnston, Susie is the geeky girl who starts school on the same day as Will. She is a small girl with rather large glasses, who also wears a blazer and a badge. Susie appears in the very first episode in the headmaster's office and the common room, then once more in the fourth episode of Series One when Neil picks her in the school's 'Blind Date' competition. In the 'Blind Date' episode, Mr Gilbert announces Susie is doing her A-Levels four years early and loves Russian literature. Anabel Barnston's other comedic credits include the BBC3 series *Coming of Age* and *Two Pints of Lager and a Packet of Crisps*. Before *The Inbetweeners*, she featured in the children's TV shows *The New Worst Witch* and *Shadow Play*.

t is for...

Tara

REPORT CARD

Music: A+ – A very keen student of music, both theory and practical.

Chemistry: E – Doesn't take well to drugs and often feels ill afterwards.

Sex Education: C – None to speak of, though not through a lack of trying!

Fashion: B – Enjoys dressing up boys, much to their discomfort.

Film and Media: C – Very fond of the *Saw* films; however, could branch out a lot more.

TARA IS PLAYED BY
HANNAH TOINTON.

BACKGROUND

Tara first appears in *The Inbetweeners* in Episode Two of Series Three and continues to appear through Episodes Three and Four. She is Simon's first real girlfriend and her love for music brings them together at a drug-fuelled rock gig.

Tara proves to be a distraction for Simon and, as their relationship blossoms, he seems to forget about his lifelong love Carli, and things are looking up for him. For Tara, Simon's *friends* are something of a distraction and seem to get in the way every time she tries to get close to him. This is apparent on the infamous trip to visit Tara's sister in Warwick, when it looks as though they will both be losing their virginity; however, his friends somehow manage to mess things up for him.

Tara is played by actress Hannah Tointon who is an English actress born on 28 December 1987. She is sister to former *EastEnders* actress and *Strictly Come Dancing* winner Kara Tointon. Before appearing in *The Inbetweeners*, Hannah made her way up the TV ladder by appearing in numerous children's television shows; however, she is most famous for playing Katy Fox in 26 episodes of the Channel 4 soap *Hollyoaks*. Her other acting credits include appearances in TV shows such as *The Bill* and *Doctors*.

Hannah's numerous scenes with Joe Thomas (Simon) proved to be the catalyst for their off-screen relationship, as they have been dating ever since meeting on the show.

FUNNIEST SCENE

Tara's funniest scene has to be at the gig. After feeling a little tipsy from all the drink and drugs, Tara decides to make a move on Simon; however, it doesn't work out entirely to plan as she throws up all over his feet! Oddly enough, rather than running away in embarrassment, she then gives Simon a whopping great kiss, not the best of first impressions!

LOVES

Simon's car
NME magazine
Failsafe

HATES

Simon's friends
Nosebleeds
Throwing up

HOBBIES

Tara is big on her music and loves going to gigs at weekends, including the Failsafe gig at The Enterprise venue, where she throws up before kissing Simon.

TARA'S PARENTS

When Simon drops Tara off from their double date at the cinema, her parents are there at the door to greet the couple. Unfortunately, Simon being Simon, he manages to make the worst of impressions with his foul mouth and scatterbrain. The practical joke Neil and Jay have played doesn't help matters either – when trying to make a good impression, the last thing you want your girlfriend's father to see is a bumper sticker on the car displaying the words 'Honk if you want a blowjob'. Needless to say the comedy sticker doesn't go down too well and Tara is swiftly taken indoors. Tara's parents are played by British actors Nick Asbury and Janine Wood, who have appeared in shows such as *The Bill*, *Doctors* and *Holby City*.

Did you know?
During the scene where Tara threw up and kissed Simon, Joe Thomas (Simon) said he could actually taste the cold vegetable soup in his mouth. The soup was used as a prop for Tara's vomit. Lovely!

Terry Cartwright (Jay's Dad)

Terry is probably the most uncompromising character in the series – it's clear to see where Jay gets his insults

HANNAH TOINTON WITH HER SISTER KARA, OF EASTENDERS AND
STRICTLY COME DANCING FAME.

and foul mouth from! Terry Cartwright's constant
belittling and humiliation of his son causes much
bewilderment for Will, Simon and Neil, as Jay fails to
answer back with his usual witty retorts, as is standard
around his friends. Altogether, Terry appears in five
episodes of the series and we first meet him during the
'Caravan Club' episode, where he announces himself
with some vigour as he manages to produce an
almighty stench in the bathroom of the caravan while
the lads are eating their dinner, after which he decides
to ridicule Jay in some fashion.

Jay's mum also appears in the show; however, she only

turns up in three episodes and very much seems to pander to her husband's needs and somewhat turns a blind eye to his cruel treatment of Jay. Mrs Cartwright is played by actress Victoria Willing. Victoria has appeared in a handful of famous British TV shows since her career took off in 1990, most notably *The Bill* and *Holby City*. Her other work includes the dramas *Wire in the Blood* and *Silent Witness*.

Terry Cartwright is played by the actor David Schaal, who also plays the character of Taffy (or Glyn) in the BBC hit series *The Office* written by Ricky Gervais and Stephen Merchant. Schaal studied drama in London and has appeared in many famous British TV shows including *Casualty*, *Doctors*, *The Bill* and *EastEnders*. Along with *The Inbetweeners* and *The Office*, his other comedy roles include appearances in Channel 4's *The IT Crowd* and *The Armando Iannucci Shows*. David is also a writer and director and has co-written a number of plays, which have appeared at the Edinburgh Festival.

LOVES
The sense of freedom you get with caravan holidays
Making a fool out of Jay

HATES
Manners
Pissing in a straight line

HOBBIES

For Terry Cartwright, there's nothing more enjoyable than a weekend away at the Caravan Club. The peace and tranquillity of it all gives him the chance to ponder life and allows him to spend some quality time with his family... and irritable bowel!

Testicles

Over the three series of *The Inbetweeners*, audiences have become very familiar with certain private parts of actor Joe Thomas (Simon) because during the school fashion show Simon walks the catwalk with one of his testicles hanging out and gives everyone an extremely close-up view!

Blake Harrison (Neil) revealed to the *Sun* that his co-star Joe is more than happy to expose himself for his art. He explains that makers of the show have even offered prosthetic testi for Joe to use but he turned them down, preferring to use the real thing. It seems Joe's more than happy to take on the most embarrassing scenes for his character Simon and, if the others show no enthusiasm for something outrageous, he will normally step up to the plate.

The appearance of Joe's bits is a running joke with the four co-stars and they regularly bring up his willingness to expose himself at interviews. James Buckley (Jay)

joked with *Digital Spy* at the British Comedy Awards that fans would see several genitalia shots in the movie... and they'd all be Joe's!

Even though Joe showed great commitment in the scenes where he had to reveal his body, he admits that he found it embarrassing. He said the fashion-show scene was the most embarrassing he was ever involved in. What made it even more uncomfortable for him was the fact that the audience weren't forewarned that he would be revealing himself in the scene and, to make them feel even more awkward, Joe was told by a dance trainer brought in for the episode to stare at as many people as possible.

Did you know?
Joe got some stick for the fashion show reveal from the other Inbetweeners, who reckon he has unusually hairy testicles!

The 11 O'Clock Show

The satirical British comedy series *The 11 O'Clock Show* aired on Channel 4 between 1998 and 2000. It was here where Iain Morris and Damon Beesley, writers of *The Inbetweeners*, would meet as producers of the show.

During its short two-year stint, the late-night show would become a hot-bed for comedy talent in the UK, catapulting actors, stand-up comedians and writers into the limelight. The most famous of the artists to emerge from *The 11 O'Clock Show* include Ricky Gervais and Sacha Baron Cohen. Gervais would go on to co-write, act in and produce some of the UK's most iconic and influential comedies such as the multi-award-winning series *The Office* and *Extras*. Baron Cohen had his own show commissioned (*Da Ali G Show*), which went on air in the UK from 2000 to 2004 and in the US (on HBO) from 2004 to 2006. He would also bring his other characters, Borat and Bruno, to both the small and big screens.

The 11 O'Clock Show took the form of a topical news programme where the two presenters, Iain Lee and Daisy Donovan, interviewed guests in the studio or from a remote location. Some of the show's presenters went on to become household names, such as Mackenzie Crook (Gareth in *The Office*), Scottish stand-up Fred MacAuley and Sarah Alexander who

HANNAH TOINTON WITH JOE SWASH.

starred in *Smack the Pony* and the sitcoms *Coupling* and *Green Wing*. Other presenters included American stand-up comic Rich Hall and British comedian Jimmy Carr, who coincidentally co-presents a similar satirical show on Channel 4: *10 O'Clock Live*.

The 11 O'Clock Show also produced an array of talented comedy writers including David Mitchell and Robert Webb, who went on to star in the award-winning comedy series *Peep Show*. Other writers included Charlie Brooker, a comedy writer and journalist whose credits include E4 zombie drama *Dead Set*, *How TV Ruined Your Life* and co-presenter with Jimmy Carr on *10 O'Clock Live*.

'The Gig and the Girlfriend': Series Three, Episode Two

This particular episode shows the Inbetweeners experimenting with drugs for the first time, while Simon gets a girlfriend.

The day starts with Jay once again talking bollocks about the girls he has apparently shagged from the playboy mansion, and meanwhile Simon is moaning about how much he wants an actual girlfriend. Funnily enough, Neil's input into the art of wooing girls seems to interest Simon: 'I read in my sister's magazine that birds like it when you ask them questions – you should try that.' It's not long before Jay pipes up with another remark: 'The only question I ask them is which hole do you want it in first?' With that, it's time to head off to school.

Local psycho Mark Donovan appears round the corner on the way there. He's smoking a joint and, as Will fumes at the sight of it, Jay remarks, 'Calm down, talk to Frank! It is only a bit of puff –the other day we got this dog stoned and it got the munchies so it ran away for an hour. When it came back, it had nicked some HobNobs from the all-night garage.' This ridiculous conversation continues for a good few minutes until Simon sees Carli and literally runs after her all the way to school and into the common room.

True to form, Carli shows no real interest in Simon. However, this proves to be his lucky day as another young lady by the name of Tara catches his eye. Tara is a year below Simon and seems to have all the attributes he looks for in a girl, so he does his best to pretend he is interested in the same things as her.

When she asks if he has been to The Enterprise to watch a gig, his reply is somewhat vague: 'Erm… The Enterprise, just trying to think… Er, can't quite…' The truth being of course not! When Tara finally prises the answer out of him, she announces that she's going to see a cool new up-and-coming band there on Friday night. Simon's response is the cardinal sin to an *NME* reader: 'Cool, I love gigs! I went to a big gig last year – my mum took us to see Take That at Wembley Arena.' Of course, that doesn't go down well with Tara, who decides the gig may not be for him, and so, in a last-ditch attempt to bring her round, he declares he will be there on the Friday and he'll be bringing the drugs with him, much to Will's dismay.

So Simon is bringing the drugs to The Enterprise on Friday night and the only question is where to get hold of the stuff. The logical answer would suggest Jay, the only one of them with apparent experience in smoking weed – 'Slight problem there, my mate has fucked off to Afghanistan on a gap year, trying to get some pure shit from the source!' However, Jay has to remain true to his word and get hold of the puff somehow, but, after he pays Mark Donovan £20 for a bag of tea, it must be elsewhere!

Friday night comes around and for some reason Simon is wearing a trilby, a new method he is using to seduce Tara. 'You look like Pete Doherty's butcher' is the comment from his dad as they get a lift to the venue. Inside The Enterprise, there is one burning issue. They still don't have any drugs – well, that's apart from Neil's sleeping pills: 'Apparently if you mix them with Ribena, red wine and cough mixture, it gives you a well-good buzz!' As Tara is expecting much more than a strange cocktail of sleep-inducing drugs, the onus is on Jay to score some weed and so off he goes.

And it works! Jay has finally come up trumps so they head outside to enjoy the fruits of his labours. After much procrastination, it's time to figure out who is to take the first puff: 'I smoked one the size of a parsnip as I was waiting for you latecomers,' claims Jay, so it's up to Simon to deliver the goods and impress Tara. But it's not his finest hour as he awkwardly takes a drag and quickly blows the smoke out. 'You have to inhale,' advises Tara. 'Yeah, I know – sometimes I do it that way as it gets your cheeks nice and stoned' is the response from Simon. After a couple of quick uncomfortable drags here and there, it's time to watch the band.

While Simon slopes off with Tara, the other three are left watching from a distance. Neil starts to feel queasy from the sleeping pills but Jay is considering getting a shipment of weed in for the Glastonbury Festival. 'Just 'cos you've had a puff on your first joint, that doesn't make you Kurt Cobain!' observes Will, a comment which angers Jay, who proceeds to call him a 'mummy's boy' and says he should have a little puff to lighten up. And so he does, but not just a puff – Will eats the whole thing and washes it down with a cold beer!

Meanwhile, Simon and Tara are enjoying the band and moshing away to the sound of Failsafe. Simon, obviously not used to correct moshing etiquette, thinks it best to get involved with the crowd aggression but goes a bit too far and pushes Tara into the front of the stage, nearly breaking her nose. However, he makes up for this by chaperoning her out of the gig area – a true gent!

While this is happening, it appears the sleeping pills have kicked in with Neil as he starts to become even more lethargic. Even weirder, he begins to break out the robot dance in slow motion. This strange behaviour has also started to rub off on Will, who is feeling the effects of the cannabis he has eaten a few moments ago: 'You need to call an ambulance right now because I can't use the phone, my arms don't work and my hands are sausages!' Jay is absolutely no help and so, with arms flailing, Will makes his way towards Neil and Simon. Unfortunately, Neil is half-asleep and Simon is too busy being thrown up on by Tara. 'Listen, Simon, this is very important information! Call an ambulance and tell them I'm in a bubble and everything is very flat – look how random my arms are. Help me!' Preoccupied with other matters, Simon promptly tells Will to fuck off and says he will have to find help elsewhere.

IN SERIES ONE, THE BOYS TAKE A MEMORABLE TRIP TO THORPE PARK.

Luckily, the band have finished so the stage is free. Will believes he will have to get help from absolutely anyone in the venue, therefore taking the microphone seems to be the only viable option: 'Hello, everyone!' The bewildered crowd look on as Will pleads onstage with rapid arm movements, going ballistic: 'I need you to call me an ambulance, or, failing that, my mummy as I think I might be dead!' Of course, he isn't dead – he just has a severe case of paranoia and, as the ambulance whisks him away, the cries of 'I want my mummy!' can still be heard.

'Thorpe Park': Series One, Episode Three

This episode takes the boys on a road trip to Thorpe Park amusement park. It starts with Simon taking driving lessons before eventually passing his test with the little help of an extremely lenient (not to mention horny!) female driving instructor.

To celebrate, Will decides a road trip is in order and, as Neil works at Thorpe Park, he convinces the lads that there are loads of birds and he can get them all free tickets. Simon being his usual self is slightly worried about the first big road trip after passing his test. Jay does his best to convince him that the car is a 'mobile pulling machine', but all Will can think about is the amount of pulley-launch roller coasters! The decisive moment comes with Neil's highly imaginative description: 'Sometimes on the rides their boobs pop out. You only get a split second of tit as they're going at about 70 miles per hour, still good, though!' The trip is on.

And so the lads set off in the yellow Cinquecento with three completely different things on their minds: girls, thrill-seeking and safety. The chase for girls begins in the first ten minutes of the journey when Jay spots a car full of muff. An increasingly agitated Simon explains that he's not going to risk everyone's neck for a few random girls and, when Jay says he would give his left bollock for them, this tips Simon over the edge and he pulls out in the middle of a funeral procession.

The trio finally arrive at Thorpe Park with two hours to go until closing time and spot more girls arriving at the same time. Simon painstakingly attempts to park the car, but Jay can't wait any longer and decides to exit the moving vehicle. His plan spectacularly backfires and to add to Simon's misery the door piles straight into a sign and on to the floor. Simon can't contain his anger and tells the others he must go home to get the car fixed. However, lucky for him, Jay explains that Neil's sister's boyfriend is a mechanic and can repair the car on the way home. Car door in hand, they step into the park.

As Will, Jay and Simon attempt to find Neil hard at work, their spirits are lifted by the sight of their friend dancing around with a wasp in his monkey costume. However, those same spirits are severely dampened when one of them has to massage Neil's naked body with sting cream. 'Fuck that!' screams Jay. 'You lot can stay here and finger Neil's arse if you want to, but I'm off to find the clunge.'

According to Jay, the 'clunge' isn't far away and can be seen heading towards the Nemesis Inferno. 'Sounds like they're thrill seekers, too,' observes Will. 'I hope they're cock seekers, too!' is the typical response from Jay. With the ride about to close, the adrenaline junkies make their way into the queue with Will convincing them the front of the ride is the best place to be and they should wait the extra half-hour to get there. Unfortunately for him, when the last ride of the day arrives, there is only one more spot available at the front. 'They've pushed in!' an outraged Will exclaims. 'Are they so dumb, they think it's OK to push in?' After a tirade of abuse, he finally agrees to sit on the remaining seat at the front next to the 'inconsiderate arseholes'… only to find three members of the Happy Foundation sitting beside him: 'I'm the worst human being in the world!'

Yellow car door in hand and Will's 'heavy sense of shame' hanging over all four of them, they walk back to the car park to reflect on a day of mixed events. After finding out that Neil's sister's boyfriend actually works at a *petrol* garage, the icing on the cake is about to land when they find the car torn to shreds in the car park. Will's barrage of abuse at the Nemesis Inferno is about to come back and haunt him as the Happy Foundation bus drives past, with the passengers flicking their middle fingers amid a series of V-signs.

Although his character Will is obsessed with roller coasters in this episode, Simon Bird actually has a phobia of rides and was extremely nervous in the days leading up to the scenes at Thorpe Park. On the day of filming, he said he felt a little queasy after riding the

roller coaster twice in a row; therefore, they had to come back months later to film him separately!

Tom

Carli's rugby-playing boyfriend is called Tom and their relationship has many ups and downs, much to the annoyance of Simon. He features for the first time at the pub during the first episode when he, Carli and Simon share an awkward drink, then at the Christmas party, where he neglects Carli for his rugby-playing mates. Lastly, he turns up in the final episode of Series Two when it seems he and Carli have split up, although in fact they are back together by the end of the series. Tom is played by Ollie Holme, whose only acting credit so far is *The Inbetweeners*.

'Trip to Warwick': Series Three, Episode Four

It's time for another eventful road trip and on this occasion it's to Tara's sister, who lives in Warwick while studying at university.

As Simon and Tara's relationship grows, the time has come for them to take the next logical step and have sex for the first time. However, in Simon's house, there are many barriers to overcome, one of them being his mum and dad who can't help but barge in whenever the lovers are together; the other being Andrew Cooper, Simon's annoying little brother. With all the distractions, the pair need to find a quiet place alone and, despite Simon's suggestion of the bushes at the bottom of his garden or his car, Tara has a better idea and that is to go and visit her sister in Warwick for the weekend so they can have 'lovely sex' together. To get them both in the mood, she suggests that Simon talks dirty to her and, after testing the waters with 'I'd like to kiss your boobs', he goes all out with the romance, telling her, 'I'm going to fuck your fucking fanny off, you twat!' It's sure to be an interesting weekend.

After telling the rest of the guys that he is finally going to have sex at the weekend, they decide that Simon needs to have a plan for when the big night arrives. Jay then tells the story of one of his mates who didn't have a plan and broke his knob in half! The tale is met with the same derision as all Jay's remarks are, and Simon decides all he needs are some condoms. 'For fuck's sake, don't wear a Johnny!' and 'It's a guaranteed hard-on killer, that's why they call it safe sex 'cos you can't get it up' is the advice on offer from Neil and Jay. Ludicrous to say the least, but strangely Simon is listening intently. 'Get her to pop the condom on with her mouth or arsehole,' continues Jay. Unsure about these wise words, Simon thinks it best they all come along and coach him through it on the day. As a bonus, Jay and Neil can tap up the campus 'clunge' while they are there. Not wanting to feel left out, Will also invites himself along, as Warwick is one of his university choices. Granted it was his last choice but it was still a choice, that was the key point!

The four lads plus Tara set off on the motorway to Warwick complete with Neil's four-litre bottle of orangeade and random bowel movements after his consumption of fast food. When they arrive in Warwick, Tara's sister Sophie seems unimpressed that Simon and all his friends have turned up expecting a party, especially when her housemate Joe already stays up all night, drinking away. Swayed by her sister, she reluctantly agrees to let them stay and says that Simon and Tara can have her room for the night: 'I don't like the idea of you having sex at all, but at least I know you're doing it somewhere comfortable.' On the surface Simon's response seems like a logical one: 'Oh absolutely, only in her vagina!'

At least they are in the house and, after finding out a Dutch girl lives there, things are maybe looking up on the chances of them getting laid, although, after Jay's last experience with a Dutch girl, maybe he's not going to be taking any chances this time around: 'When I fingered her, she shit down my arm!' Heike from Holland is surely in for one hell of a night...

Sophie's flatmate Joe has invited his friends around, or as he calls them the 'Commander' and 'Bombardier', so this is an ideal opportunity for Will to sample university life. As he tries to enter into the banter, he is immediately handed a can of lager. 'Get it down you, Zulu warrior!' is the unusual cry from the Admiral and his crewmembers. It's not long before Will, Jay and Neil are also thrust into the drinking games.

Elsewhere, Simon can't keep his hands off Tara and is furiously dry-humping her in the kitchen. After suggesting they go upstairs, he first seeks advice from Jay, much to his girlfriend's annoyance. His problem is that he can't control his 'excitement' and, if she touches it once, it's sure to go off! Jay suggests a quick tactical wank to curb his enthusiasm when the big moment arrives. A good idea, thinks Simon, as he quickly heads upstairs to 'knock one out' and, even weirder, as he is doing it, he decides to sniff his girlfriend's sister's knickers at the same time!

Downstairs, the Admiral and the crew are still drinking away. To make matters worse, Neil has started drinking from his orangeade bottle complete with cigarette butts and random drink mixtures. However grotesque this is, it seems to secure the admiration of the drinking crew. To avoid having to take on the 'boring' tag, Will decides to start eating a bonsai tree to increase his social standing within the group, and this is not his finest moment, to say the least!

Meanwhile, Simon is having problems with Tara in the bedroom. Thinking back to Jay's advice in school, he asks Tara to put on the condom to spice things up a notch. However, after the episode with Sophie's knickers in the bathroom, it seems he's not quite ready yet, so Simon makes the suggestion all girls want to hear: 'I think it would help my readiness if you put it on with your mouth or your bum.' So that's exactly what she does, but, regrettably for Simon, it's still not working!

The other three have finally had enough of drink and bonsai trees so they trot off to bed and, as Will and Neil lay romantically in a single bed together, suddenly there is a feeling of warmth. Unfortunately, it's not body heat but Neil pissing the bed while he sleeps! Will frantically jumps out of bed and then wakes his friend up. 'Stop it; stop pissing!' comes the cry from the briefcase one. 'It's good for you,' says Neil as he wakes, trying to manage both his piss and a banging headache. 'Oh right, so I'll piss on you then, shall I? Get the fuck to the toilet!'

While this is happening, Jay is trying to seduce an extremely frightened Dutch girl and Simon is doing his best not to scare Tara by taking his anger out on his flaccid penis: 'Why won't you get big? Oh please, just work, you ugly cunt!' Surely this is how the two friends imagined their first time? With the threat of the police on the way, Will, the sex pest, the bed wetter and self-abuser are all subsequently ordered to leave the house at once.

After spending the night in the car, they make their way home the next day, half-naked and hungover. While Jay throws up in a plastic bag, the forecasted text comes through from Tara never to call her again.

U is for...

University Students

The university students feature in the 'Trip to Warwick' episode when Tara invites Simon to her sister's house, although what Tara didn't bank on was Will, Jay and Neil tagging along, too. The students consist of Sophie, Heike, Joe, Lewis and Daniel.

Sophie is Tara's rather protective and downbeat sister, who reluctantly agrees to let the couple stay in her bed, but only if they are safe and Simon showers beforehand. She is played by Charlie Covell, who has appeared in various TV shows including *Doctors*, *Midsomer Murders* and *Law & Order: UK*.

Heike is Sophie's Dutch housemate, who has flu at

the times of the lads' visit. Neil and Jay take an instant liking to her and, after Jay's experience with girls from Holland, he decides to make a drunken move later in the episode. Heike is played by Ambrosine Falck and her only other TV appearance is as a cyborg in the short fantasy drama *Hollow Feet* (2009).

Joe also lives in the house with Sophie and Heike. Sophie dislikes him to some extent because of his regular drinking sessions in the house with his drinking buddies. Known as the 'Admiral', the 'Commander' and the 'Bombardier', all three play drinking games with Jay, Neil and Will before heading off to the union for more pints. Joe is played by Jack Brear, an actor who appeared in many theatre productions before landing his first TV role in *The Inbetweeners*.

Joe's drinking friends are Lewis and Daniel, otherwise known as the 'Commander' and 'Bombardier', who arrive at the house ready for typical student drinking games. Lewis is played by Lewis Linford, whose biggest TV role to date is a recurring part in the long-running ITV series *Emmerdale* (2008/09). Daniel is played by Daniel Kirrane, who started his TV acting career in 2007 with a small part in another E4 series *Skins*. Since then, he has taken roles in various TV shows such as *Doctors*, *Casualty* and *Hustle*. In 2010, Daniel was the star of Visa's FIFA World Cup advertising campaign in which he played the part of a man running through various continents and ending up scoring a goal in a football stadium. Before and during the 2010 World Cup in South Africa, the campaign garnered praise and critical acclaim for its impact and innovation.

BLAKE HARRISON HAS A CLOSE ENCOUNTER.

Unseen Characters

Technically speaking, the head of the school Mr Hopkins is seen in the show... but only the back of his head very briefly and a view of part of his face from a distance in one of the first few scenes. He did have a scene deleted in which he greeted all of the school's newcomers but, in the actual series, he never has a speaking part. He is, however, mentioned on a handful of occasions.

Neil's sister's boyfriend Dave lives with the family but is never seen in the series. It is mentioned in the first series ('Thorpe Park' episode) that he is a mechanic and will be able to fix Simon's car; however, it turns out that he only works in a petrol station. Dave also helps Neil to fix up a new car before the infamous trip to London and it is mentioned that, as he is finding an engine for the car, Simon will have to drive.

In the last episode of the series, Neil announces that he is to become a father – he has got a girl pregnant after she was being very saucy at the cheese counter. In Neil's phone she is known as 'Saucy ASDA Karen'. However, in the end the test result she referred to was a Chlamydia test and so Neil will not be a father after all.

Steve D'Amato (Carli's father) is never seen in the series, although he is mentioned on a handful of occasions, most notably when Simon breaks into Carli's house in the middle of the night and the next day threatens to 'fuck him up' if he goes near the place again. Mrs D'Amato (Carli's mum) is seen only briefly in the 'Bunk Off' episode when Jay, Neil and Simon wait for Will to come out of the off-licence. Jay shouts something at her, along the lines of 'He wants to suck your Carli's tits!', following which she glances back but doesn't seem to hear exactly what was said.

Sadie Cunningham is a member of Jay's registration class. She is never seen in the series, although she is mentioned on a couple of occasions as Jay often steals things from her bag. In the 'Will's Birthday' episode, Jay steals a flyer for a party at Louise Graham's house and, in the 'Duke of Edinburgh Awards' episode, he steals some hair-removal cream from her bag, which is later used on Will as a comedy prank.

Jay mentions he has a mate named Chris Groves in the first episode of Series Two, the 'Field Trip' episode. Chris is in the year above Jay and apparently tells him that, every year on the geography field trip, there is an older woman who has sex with one person from the school. Chris allegedly was the chosen one on last year's trip and says it was the best he has ever had, or to quote Chris Groves through the medium of Jay: 'A right fit mature bird that does it because she loves young meat!'

In the 'Home Alone' episode, Neil mentions he has a cousin. This comes about as Simon is dressed in his golf attire and Neil observes that his cousin dressed the same way for a job interview. When Simon asks if he also plays golf, of course the natural response from Neil is: 'No, he's got Down's syndrome!'

Sarah Bell and Jo Larkin's voices can both be heard in the first episode of Series Three at the fashion show. When Neil is desperate to see the girls getting dressed behind the curtain, he tells Simon what he would like to see: 'I reckon Sarah Bell has got lovely big nipples and I bet Jo Larkin shaves her pubes!' After that, the girls' voices pipe up, expressing their disgust at Neil's pervy comments. When Jay arrives, he tells Simon and Neil a story of how during the school play they managed to cut a hole through the curtain and were getting 'noshed off' in between scenes. Either Sarah's or Jo's voice pipes up again to instantly dismiss Jay's make-believe tale.

During the school fashion show, Charlotte explains that Paul Keenan was supposed to be modelling with her but got so nervous that he drank a bottle of vodka and passed out in the staff toilets. She asks for Will's help in replacing him on the catwalk and he gladly obliges.

It is mentioned that Jay has a sister in the final episode of Series One, but she is never seen. Her name remains unknown but Will uses her to get back at Jay after he says Charlotte only pulled him for a bet.

During the fashion show, Carli requires Simon to fill

EMILY ATACK HITS THE TOWN WITH LIZZIE CUNDY.

in for Chris Yates for the sexy finale (she sacked him for having a 'disgustingly hairy back'). Simon agrees, and the rest is history!

Unseen Footage

There is plenty of unaired *Inbetweeners'* footage available, if you look around for it. The majority of unseen film and deleted scenes was cut from the final edit of the series, mainly due to the time constraints of cutting the show for a half-hour episode. However, some of the deleted scenes have produced comedy moments in their own right and often provide shots and insights that you don't get to see in the series. The deleted scenes that follow can all be found on the DVD special features from each series.

One of the unaired scenes from the first episode of Series One involves Will and some other kids who are also starting at Rudge Park Comprehensive in the head teacher's office. The head sits next to Mr Gilbert and assures them about the school bullying policy while handing out name badges. Coincidentally, the head never appears in the final cut of the series, although he is mentioned on a handful of occasions. In addition to the scene in the head's office, when Simon and Will walk up the stairwell in the school and Simon tells Will to take off his badge due to the threat of being bullied, the head can be heard on the school loudspeaker telling Will to put the badge back on! This scene was later replaced for a much simpler version without the head's voice and in one corridor rather than the stairs.

Some unseen footage from Series Two involves a lot more extended scenes that never made the final cut: for example, in the 'Work Experience' episode when Will finds Charlotte working at the bar for the under-eighteens disco. There is around a minute's dialogue between the pair, which was never seen – the footage shows Charlotte and Will flirting with each other just before Wolfie arrives to spoil the party. Another extended scene involves Neil at Will's dinner party when he goes into more detail about the type of small plastic toy building bricks he could put up his bum when he was younger! Another bit of unseen footage from the London trip episode includes the initial introduction of the tramp. After the gang park the car and make their way to the club, the tramp can be seen in an alleyway and he's urinating on the shoes that Simon wears later on in the episode. In the final cut, the tramp simply tells Simon that the shoes are covered in his piss. Other extra, unseen footage from the second series includes Will's mum walking into Will's bedroom as he tries to show Simon that his pubes have fallen out and Jay's dad making sickening remarks when meeting his girlfriend Chloe.

Before Series Three, a short prequel was made that never got into the first episode. This included what the boys had been up to over the summer period, how they were looking forward to the new term and reflected on the previous year, with most of that reflection being about Will shitting himself at the end-of-year exams. Some scenes from Series Three that were never aired include Tara getting aggravated at a man after Simon tells her that he was the one who pushed her into the front barrier at the gig. We also find out that Neil's middle name is Lindsay after his dad makes a speech at his eighteenth birthday party. In the Warwick episode, there is a scene where the 'Admiral', 'Commander' and 'Bombardier' discuss with Jay in detail that Heike is a nymphomaniac. However, in the episode itself this is only mentioned in passing. In another deleted scene involving Will and his mum, while they discuss the ins and outs of her dirty weekend, we get a glimpse of the flower arrangement that Jay and Neil vandalised to display the words 'We Come Tit Village'. In the episode itself, the flowers are only visible after the vandalism during the end montage.

V is for...

Vests

'Scrambled eggs and disappointment' – as Will wanders downstairs for his seventeenth birthday, his mum greets him in the kitchen with a cooked breakfast and a sleeveless surprise. When Will opens the gift, he sees two little words that bring excitement to many teenagers growing up: 'Calvin Klein'. Unfortunately, on this occasion a tight black vest isn't exactly what he had hoped for. After explaining to his mum that he isn't in a boy band, she somehow manages to persuade him to wear the vest for his birthday party, and what happens when Will wears the birthday vest is a series of unfortunate events leading to humiliation.

Virginity

Losing their virginity is the Holy Grail for all four of the Inbetweeners. It's the constant and mostly unsuccessful pursuit of girls that lands the boys in some of the best situations of the show but, despite constant efforts to pop their cherries, their goal remains further away than ever for some of the lads.

Although Jay claims to be very experienced in the bedroom department with a repertoire that includes threesomes and Caravan Club orgies, his bullshit tales don't fool anyone (well, maybe they fool Neil!). For Jay, losing his 'V-plates' came 'many suck-jobs ago' and he takes great pride in 'coaching' the others to lose theirs.

Will gets a golden opportunity to break the habit of a lifetime early in Series One when the popular and promiscuous Charlotte 'Big Jugs' Hinchcliffe invites him over to her house. Will decides it's best not to share his lack of experience, so he tells Charlotte that he's had numerous conquests but, when the pair get under the covers, Will's virginity is quickly apparent. He's subsequently kicked out, still a virgin, having only rubbed 'up against the perineum'. But he gets another chance when the guys go to the Caravan Club with Jay. Here, a punk girl advances on the geeky and nervous Will. Again, he messes up his chances, though – this time not even getting as far as the bed sheets. Nerves get the better of him and, instead of leaving the disco with the girl, Will takes to the dance floor, where he skids around like a five-year-old. Obviously, this doesn't impress the girl and she leaves him to it. Luckily for her, Neil is around to pick up the pieces and they spend the night together in Simon's car.

But this isn't the only time when Neil swoops in after Will. After Will dumps 'Big Kerry' at Neil's eighteenth, Neil later reveals that he managed to get a blowjob from her and, when Will fails to make an impression on Charlotte, Neil again strikes lucky. Neil's other conquest of the show is with an older woman working on the cheese counter at ASDA. After having sex, Neil thinks he's got her pregnant only to find out later that the test she's had is for Chlamydia, not a baby! Although Neil is the most experienced of all the lads, all his sexual encounters are off-camera and only revealed after they happen.

Simon is the complete opposite on the show. His romances, including his relentless chasing of Carli and the short relationship with Tara, are played out onscreen. Losing his virginity with Carli is something he can only dream of, but he gets much closer to the main event with Tara when the pair travel to Warwick to visit her sister for the weekend. The only problem is that, after following Jay's advice on having a pre-sex fumble with himself, Simon loses the ability to perform and, like his best mate Will with Charlotte, is kicked out of the bedroom.

Vomit

Vomiting is one of the more unpleasant parts of growing up and it's no different for the Inbetweeners. When the guys decide to bunk off school for the day and opt for a drinking session at Neil's house, they go a bit overboard on the booze. Having already downed a bottle of gin with the others, Simon drinks a cocktail created by Jay to give him a better chance of impressing Carli.

After drinking all day, Simon feels the effects and vomits all over Carli's kitchen and little brother! In order to get such an effective projectile vomit, the makers of the show devised a cunning plan: a device was fashioned out of a pump with a tube running up actor Joe Thomas's back and filled with vegetable soup!

In 'The Making Of' from Series One, Emily Head (Carli) explains that she has had the unfortunate experience of people being sick on her many times. Joe Thomas says he's normally sick on himself, unlike his character Simon who seems to vomit on everyone but himself!

Carli isn't the only love interest involved in a vomiting scene with Joe. Series Three co-star Hannah Tointon (Tara) said her vomiting scene with him was the most embarrassing she had to play. Joe even admitted to being able to taste the cold vegetable soup during the kissing scene with Tara that followed! He did well to make it through the scene without flinching, but the same cannot be said for James Buckley (Jay), who felt the effects during filming of the vomiting frenzy inside a tent for the final episode of the third series. Buckley said, 'Even though I knew it was vegetable soup and it was all over us, someone had to get me a little bowl and I had to be sick.'

Vegetable soup and real sick, what a combination!

W is for...

West Ham

Throughout the three series of *The Inbetweeners*, serial bullshitter Jay Cartwright references his junior football career at West Ham. We're first introduced to his playing career in the first series when Will gets a girlfriend. When the Inbetweeners are at a house party, they notice Jay talking to someone outside the foursome. After questioning him about the stranger, he tells them that he's just a friend from when he had trials at the London club.

Simon says, 'He's just a friend from when Jay had trials at West Ham that never happened!'

The gang continue to give Jay stick about his 'fwend'

until he eventually cracks and ends up jumping up and down all over the innocent guy's car.

Another of Jay's reminiscences about his playing career at West Ham comes when the guys head off to Warwick for Simon's best chance yet of losing his virginity with new girlfriend Tara. After the gang finds out that Tara's sister shares a house with a Dutch student, Jay tells them about the reputation of European girls.

He claims he found out about this reputation on a West Ham under-13s football tour to Holland. When prompted into explaining what actually happened, he provides one of his most outlandish tales of the whole series: 'When I fingered her, she shit down my arm!' He goes on to tell Neil that Dutch girls are 'filthy, they're hairy… and they don't mind if you wipe it on the curtains!' Even for Jay these are pretty risqué comments and he leaves the other lads absolutely dumbstruck. Rather than questioning his 'career' at West Ham any further, they quickly change the subject.

'Briefcase Wanker' Will Mackenzie is played by Simon Bird.

Will

REPORT CARD

Sex Education: F – Will has yet to prosper in this subject. The only piece of work he has produced was with former pupil Charlotte 'Big Jugs' Hinchcliffe and the quality was so poor it couldn't even be marked.

French: F – Will initially showed great promise in this area when he welcomed a French exchange student; however, this quickly turned to hatred so he must be given a fail.

PE: F – Sport is obviously not Will's strong point and, after he threw a Frisbee at a disabled girl's face, this mark is justified.

Other Languages: F – Will needs to understand that impressions of Yoda from Star Wars do not constitute other languages and only annoy and alienate pupils.

Business Studies: A+ – Will's running of the Xmas Prom event shows he has great management potential.

BACKGROUND

Described by his nearest and dearest as 'Wanker', 'Briefcase Wanker' and 'Virgin', Will McKenzie is probably best liked for his fit mum and is what can only be described as completely socially inept, so he obviously starts off the story of *The Inbetweeners*.

Following his parents' break-up, Will is taken out of

the security of his plush private education and forced to attend 'normal school': Rudge Park Comprehensive. Along with the 'newcomers' badge he's forced to wear, the briefcase and private-school background, Will's Inbetweener position within the school is quickly established, leaving him few options on the friend front – 'stick with the freaks, or try to make friends with the guy [Simon] they now call boner' – and, because beggars can't be choosers, Will decides that Simon, Neil and Jay are his best option.

Throughout the series, Will remains closest to Simon in the group. This is probably because he was the first one to take him under his wing, but also because Simon and Will are the only two in the group who seem able to hold a slightly intelligent conversation.

Like all the Inbetweeners, Will isn't known for his luck with the ladies. His romantic encounters include a forced date with 'Big Kerry', skidding around the dance floor at Caravan Club and his pursuit of the popular Charlotte 'Big Jugs' Hinchcliffe.

Charlotte is the biggest love interest of Will's life at Rudge Park. Although he gets close to losing his virginity with the school sexpert, lack of any knowledge or rhythm in that area lead to what can only be described as an un-rhythmic, awkward and very brief encounter. Quite literally, a fish out of water!

FUNNIEST SCENE

Will's most amusing scene has to be when, thanks to a tonne of energy drink and caffeine tablets, he loudly loses all control of his bowels during an exam in front of a hall full of pupils. This leaves him wearing a pair of pants and tracksuit bottoms from Lost Property, while carrying his soiled school uniform in a plastic bag!

LOVES

Briefcases
Private school
Coq au vin
Dinner parties
Frisbee

HATES

Comprehensive school
Mark Donovan
People leering over his fit mum
People asking if he'd shag his mum
French people tugging over his mum
Thorpe Park

HOBBIES

Will loves nothing more than a friendly game of Frisbee down the local park. Not known for his sporting prowess, he can certainly throw a Frisbee around, though. That's until Episode Two of Series One when, in an attempt to grab the attention of Carli and her friends, he accidentally hits a wheelchair-bound woman on the head with his Frisbee. As expected, comedy chaos ensues including a rant from the victim's Polish friend. Will attempts to take back his Frisbee – after all, he does own the thing and has a receipt to prove it. Needless to say, he doesn't get the Frisbee back and ends up being chased by Mark Donovan instead.

Unlike other first-year sixth-formers whose typical night out includes ten pints and a kebab, Will prefers an evening of good food, wine and intellectual conversation. In Episode Three of Series Two, he decides to put his hosting skills to the test and invites the other Inbetweeners and all of the girls he 'knows' to a birthday dinner party in his honour. Not only do Simon, Neil and Jay think the evening is 'bollocks', but the girls also prefer the option of a cooler party.

Every teenager likes a theme park and with Episode Three in Series One comes the visit to Thorpe Park. The trip's going relatively well (apart from Neil losing his clothes and Simon losing a door!) and, after spending over an hour queuing for the Nemesis, Will's love of parks quickly crumbles. Ready-to-front-row Will starts another rant when told he can't have the seat he wants. What he doesn't know is that it's been given to a group of disabled teenagers... leaving him looking like a terrible human being!

> *Did you know?*
> Rather than admitting he's joined a state comprehensive, Will tells his old school friends that he's doing voluntary work for UNICEF. If only Jay knew!

'Girlfriend': Series One, Episode Four

It's Saturday night and the Inbetweeners are at fellow pupil Wendy's house party, 'bored senseless and wondering how they'll ever get laid'. Despite the grim start, things begin to look up when Wendy mentions that cool kid Charlotte 'Big Jugs' Hinchcliffe and her friends may make an appearance. On hearing the news, Jay reveals that he's heard rumours she's a slag who once 'munched off the whole rugby team' – although Will points out their school doesn't even have a rugby team!

This is when we're introduced to Jay's 'fwend'. The group are shocked that Jay knows anyone outside their unpopular group and, when he explains that it's just a guy he met while doing trials at West Ham, they start to make fun of him – 'fwend, football fwend!'

The boys' attention wanes as Charlotte 'Big Jugs' walks in, making this officially the coolest party they've ever been to. They decide its best to try to look cool, so all strike a pose at Charlotte and her mates. As you'd expect, they don't impress and the girls laugh at the hapless hopefuls.

While the others are making fools of themselves, Will is on the hunt for some more alcohol. He stumbles across a bottle of champagne only to discover that it's Charlotte's. Surprisingly, she asks him to join her for a drink and, despite him trying to impress her with facts about the original design of the champagne glass (based on Marie Antoinette's breast), his luck seems to be in.

Jay finds Will and Charlotte chatting in the kitchen and, in a ploy to impress her, decides to show her his 'crazy frog' impression. She sticks with Will and, after the two have been chatting for a while, leads him to a bedroom upstairs.

With Will and Charlotte in the bedroom, Charlotte's ex-boyfriend (and school bully) Mark Donovan arrives. Immediately, he heads upstairs and walks in to find the pair kissing but, thanks to Charlotte, Will is spared a beating.

After the party finishes, the four still can't believe Will's good fortune with Charlotte. Back at school, he continues on a winning streak as she calls him over for a talk. The topic quickly gets on to sex and, after finding out that Charlotte's very experienced in the department, Will decides it's best to tell a white lie about his sexual experiences (*five* white lies, actually):'one was a couple of weeks ago, another one was a few days ago'. Impressed by his apparent expertise, Charlotte invites him round that Friday for sex.

On Will's big day, he gets all dressed up and goes over to Charlotte's. The big moment arrives, but his inexperience soon shows itself. She quickly ends the encounter and tells Will he can't count it as losing his virginity – even he only describes it as 'rubbing up against the perineum'!

Neil decides lying may be the best way for him to get a girl, too. Rather than wasting time at parties chasing disinterested girls, he decides to enter the school's 'Blind Date' show. Ever the confused, he chooses Susie, a pupil who started at the same time as Will and who is studying for her A-Levels four years early, which makes her around twelve – not quite the type of person he had hoped to meet! On the same show, Charlotte breaks Will's heart by also appearing as a contestant.

At least Simon and Jay try to make Will feel better with the episode ending as they go off to watch Neil and his date (and her mum!) eat a Bargain Bucket at a chicken restaurant.

'Will's Birthday': Series Two, Episode Three

The episode kicks off in the common room of Rudge Park Comprehensive with Neil attempting to exercise his limited mental ability on a brain game only to be given the score of a twelve-year-old! Jay shows Neil and the others who is really the brains behind the gang when he announces that they're going to schoolmate Louise Grahams' 'Sexy Soiree' on Saturday. For a split second it looks as if the Inbetweeners may have actually been invited to a cool party until Jay reveals that he stole the invite from a girl's bag during registration.

BELINDA STEWART-WILSON WITH FORMER HUSBAND BEN MILLER.

Anyway, the boys don't need to worry because, despite it slipping their minds, Will (in his typically mature, sophisticated and boring way!) has planned a dinner party for his birthday. Despite the others being less than enthusiastic about his plans because they'd all rather try to bunk into Louise's party, Will manages to convince the guys to come, reminding them to bring girls, too. But, rather than bring a date (unlikely, considering his luck with the ladies!), Simon tells the group that if he goes then he will have to bring along the French exchange student staying with him, too.

Back at Simon's house, the guys meet Patrice, a chain-smoking, flock haired, leather-jacket-wearing exchange student. Then back at Will's house, along with an uninterested Simon and Patrice, Will looks for recipes for his dinner party in a poor attempt to impress the ladies. He decides on the classic Coq au Vin. While looking for ideas, his internet messenger pops up to announce Charlotte is online – the girl Will attempted to lose his virginity with in the first series.

Despite the disaster of his last encounter with Charlotte, Simon convinces Will to start a conversation with her – and all is going well with plenty of smiley faces, LOLs and cheeky banter until he plucks up the courage to ask her to his dinner party on Saturday. After a painful wait, the dreaded message pops up: 'Charlotte is Offline'.

Like all the boys, Patrice takes an immediate liking to Will's mum, and for the first time she seems to take an interest, too. It's an awkward moment as the pair gaze at each other with Will's mum giggling away and Will mortified by her behaviour.

The next day it's Will's birthday and time for his big gift. Like most seventeen-year-olds, Will has his heart set on a car but his mum has other ideas – a tight vest top – and, although Will is hardly known for his fashion sense, this one seems dodgy even for him! Rather than disappointing his mum, Will promises to wear it that night, though.

The evening of the dinner party gets off to a bad start (for Will, anyway) with Patrice deciding to tell him: 'I've just had a really nice tug, thinking about your mother. I think some went on the floor, sorry!' Things don't get any better as Jay and Neil arrive without any girls. That leaves the four Inbetweeners, a French exchange student and a Coq au Vin – a crap party, even by Will's standards. Jay and Neil then decide to reveal they've ordered a stripper, letting the others know they all need to chip in.

After several more failures of the night, including being called a 'paedo' by a group of young drunk girls, a stripper turning up to the house to be greeted by Will's confused mum and a failed attempt to run away from Patrice, the Inbetweeners and the French exchange student eventually end up going to Louise's party.

The five arrive to a packed house, including Will's love interest Charlotte 'Big Jugs' Hinchcliffe. Even Big John appears to be getting some action and it finally seems as if things are looking up. But, apart from the good-looking Patrice, they are all turned away at the door. Undeterred, they decide to climb the back fence to get to the 'clunge'. Not known for his athletic ability, Will opts to crawl through a gap in the fence but ends up covered in dog shit. Two things come out of this move: Louise decides to let the desperate no-hopers stay on at the party and Will is forced to take his stinking jacket off, leaving him in his tight birthday vest – not a good look!

Will decides not to let fashion get in the way and goes on the hunt for Charlotte. Neil recommends looking in the bedrooms, saying she'll 'probably be shagging' up there. No surprise when he's proved right and Will walks into one of the rooms to find her with Patrice!

It's another momentous end to a failed night for the Inbetweeners – and definitely not the evening Will had planned.

Did you know?
Blake Harrison (Neil) described the dinner party at Will's as 'one of my favourite scenes' and he explained how the boys were constantly being told off for messing about and laughing throughout the filming. Maybe it was the tight vest Simon Bird had to wear, described by James Buckley (Jay) as 'A sixty-year-old ex-wrestler'!

'Will's Dilemma': Series Three, Episode Three

In this episode, Will gets an opportunity to double date with Simon, Tara and one of her friends.

It begins with the lads drooling over Neil's eighteenth-birthday present: a new motorbike. Not for long, however, as Jay manages to successfully smash it into a wall and writes it off. That's that, and now the only present Neil has left is a birthday party arranged for him, which all the lads were planning to attend… if only for the sight of his fit sister!

Simon breaks the news to Will that they will be going on a double date to the cinema with Tara and her friend Kerry. Will seems highly disgruntled by the news, especially not knowing what the girl in question looks like, but, after finding out that Kerry has given her last three boyfriends blowjobs, he quickly agrees to attend.

The double date begins at the shopping centre and Kerry is probably one of the tallest girls Will has ever seen, so naturally he takes a dislike to her. Soon they are left to pair off as Tara has her eye on a special outfit for Simon to wear – more specifically, shorts, a check shirt, bow-tie, a pink cardigan and glasses. It's the sort of geek chic that Simon is far from comfortable about; however, with the prospect of sex on the cards, it's got to be worth it!

In the meantime, Will has a dilemma on his hands and, when he tries to explain to Simon that Kerry is a giant, his friend quickly reminds him that he doesn't have anything else on the cards and her past experiences with blowjobs should stand him in good stead to get one, if he sticks with it. In order to make up his mind, Will takes some bad advice from Jay and Neil, who are hiding around the corner in the shopping centre: 'I got my first blowjob from the cleaner when I was twelve – it was brilliant, I pissed right in her mouth!' With that unpleasant description, it's time for the second leg of their double date: the cinema.

In the cinema, Kerry does her best to help Will overcome his fear of scary films by putting her massive hands around him. Unsure if it's because of the hands or the film, Will faints and becomes the laughing stock of the room – and not for the first time! After the trauma of the cinema, Big Kerry walks him home and, as standard at the end of the night, they kiss (or, rather, she picks him up and slaps one on his lips before he runs inside!).

In school the next day, all the talk is about Will and Kerry's kiss and how she has changed her Facebook status to 'In a relationship'. When questioned about it, Will is still uncertain about the situation but, after much deliberation and the search for that elusive blowjob, he decides to plod on with Kerry and see where it leads, not to mention the fact that Neil's party is around the corner and he needs to boost the numbers.

The party is turning out to be a washout and the only thing to smile about so far is Simon's new outfit and the sight of Neil's incredibly attractive sister. As the guests arrive, it's turning out to be one of the worst eighteenth-birthday parties in history! Fortunately for Simon, Neil allows him to take Tara upstairs, leaving Will alone with Kerry. Sitting with his new 'girlfriend', Will decides that it's time to let her down gently; however, by 'gently' he means telling her: 'I don't want to be your boyfriend and if anyone asks I never was!' Not quite how it was meant to come out and it sends her into floods of tears and accusations of how Will has only used her for blowjobs. Soon he is asked to leave the party: 'Why, for turning down oral sex from the Empire State Building?' Even after pleading his innocence, Will leaves in disgrace.

Some good comes from the party, however: Neil *did* manage to get several blowjobs from Kerry after the guests had left… Apparently, there were still a few tears during the first one!

Wolfie

Seventeen-year-old Wolfie is a mechanic who works with Will at the garage during 'Work Experience'. He seems as though he should be about thirty, though, due to his beard and general demeanour. As soon as Will arrives at the garage, Wolfie and his mechanic friends set about playing pranks on him because of his posh behaviour and general talking down to them. In the end, Wolfie manages to throw Will into a lake and messes up his chances with Charlotte in one week. Wolfie is played by David Fynn, an English actor and producer who has appeared in many popular British dramas, including *Doctor Who*, *Spooks* and *Doctors*. He has also had a part in the award-winning Channel 4 series *Peep Show*. Along with TV appearances, Fynn has worked on a Foster's Lager commercial, where he asks two Australian men for their advice on whether his girlfriend will look like her mother in the future. He is also keen behind the camera, producing and directing internet-based sketch shows and mock documentaries.

'Work Experience': Series Two, Episode Two

This episode finds the boys at work experience – an exciting time for all teenagers because they get to experience life away from the school gates for the first time. This is especially true for geeky Will as it's the perfect opportunity to hone his journalism skills in a local newspaper office. Unfortunately for him, due to an administration error (and much to the delight of Mr Gilbert), Will's and Neil's applications were mixed up, thereby placing him at a garage for two whole weeks rather than the newspaper. Despite Neil's admission that he has never wanted to work at a newspaper or ever read one, the decision made by Gilbert is to stick to the original plans.

The 'Work Experience' day episode also falls on the same day as Valentine's Day and, as the lads await their work experience fate, Jay shares with them what is written in some of the cards he received: 'Roses are red, violets are blue, your dong is massive, I want to blow you, love your secret slut' reads one of the cards, which all look suspiciously similar to Jay's handwriting. As if to hammer home the bullshit, Will reads out another card: 'Jay, you massive stud, please, please spaff on my face from your Valentine's bitch'.

Luckily, romance hasn't been lost on everyone: Neil hands Will a Valentine to give to his mum later, Simon has received a card from a girl in the year below, and Will has sent a bouquet of flowers to Charlotte 'Big Jugs' Hinchcliffe. Naturally, Charlotte thinks this a grand gesture and has invited Will to keep her company while she works behind the bar at an under-eighteens disco – result!

Speaking of under-eighteens, while Jay and Simon ponder their fortnight of work experience at Jay's dad's

In 'Work Experience', Neil's and Will's applications get mixed up and Neil ends up working on a newspaper.

building firm, they bump into Danny Moore – a young kid from the rough end of Northwood. It seems he doesn't take kindly to the lads calling him a short arse and so he sets about planning to do Simon in at the earliest opportunity. A fight with a twelve-year-old Northwood character doesn't interest Simon in the slightest, much to the delight of Jay and Neil, who proceed to goad him by calling him a chicken.

When the first day of work experience arrives, Will goes along to the garage with a sense of optimism, safe in the knowledge that he'll be where he belongs (i.e. at the local paper) the very next day. He doesn't get off to the best of starts, though, for, after meeting with his new colleagues, Jim, Steve and the ridiculously old-looking seventeen-year-old Wolfie, Will starts to dig his own grave: 'No offence, but I'm never going to work in a place like this. It's not that I'm better than this, it's just that I'm much cleverer than you need to be to work here!' It's a move he'll later regret as Wolfie and the guys spot the perfect opportunity to taunt the posh kid. After they have asked 'Chumley Warner' for supplies of tartan paint, spirit level bubbles and a reach around, Will's initiation ceremony is to happen at lunchtime.

After a well-earned lunchtime pint bonding with his garage colleagues, Will feels a lot more at ease with his new manual-labour friends – that is until they decide to bundle him into the back of a car with his pants down and throw him into a lake! This prompts Will's mum to take action and, with Neil's dad in tow, she pays a visit to the school. She explains to Mr Gilbert, head of sixth form, that her son has had to walk back through the town centre sopping wet and barely clothed, but the thought of this leaves the Gilbert failing to contain his laughter and Neil's dad in somewhat of a trance.

As the week goes on, it's fast approaching Will's 'date' with Charlotte, and Jay, Simon and Neil realise they have nothing better to do than to tag along and watch Will make a fool of himself at the under-eighteens disco. As always, Jay has other agendas, though – best summed up in the sentence: 'If there's grass on the pitch, play ball!'

Before his Friday-night date, Will has to endure what he thinks is his last day at the garage, so as a swansong he thinks it's best to join in the camaraderie and banter. He decides to tell all about the lovely Charlotte: 'She's fit, she's older than me and she goes like a porn star!' So, on hearing that laddish description, Wolfie, the seventeen-year-old trapped in a thirty-year-old's body, decides to come along to the disco, too. Brilliant!

At the disco (or Will's 'date' as he keeps referring to it), there doesn't seem to be a single person over the age of fourteen, so it's hardly an ideal place for four sixth-form students to be hanging out. However, Simon is to see the first bit of action during the night when Valentine Hannah from the year below approaches him for a drink and a dance. After he agrees, he gets more than he bargains for on a very well-lit dance floor. 'The jammy git's only gone and pulled an experienced cock handler!' screams Jay. 'Thanks to me, we're now watching Simon get wanked off!' The boys continue to watch Simon on the dance floor but they also observe Danny Moore stepping into the room and subsequently kicking their friend in the cock. A child has beaten up Simon and, what's more, he's told all his Northwood mates! Unfortunately for Will, Jay and Neil, they are about to feel the wrath, too.

Luckily, Will has a plan and decides to find Charlotte to get the Northwood hooligans kicked out while the others hide in the toilets. Unfortunately for him, while talking with Charlotte at the bar, he is joined by Wolfie from the garage, who immediately tells her about Will's derogatory language towards her at work, which prompts an iced soft drink to be poured over Will and the meanest of cold shoulders!

Not only are the three others being humiliated in a toilet cubicle, they have to deal with Neil taking a piss sitting down (which he apparently does as a treat, every now and again). As Will arrives to save the day, the DJ smugly announces, 'William McKenzie's mother is here at the front door to pick him and his three friends up.'

Another tragic night is topped off by the sound of laughing fourteen-year-olds!

Writers – Iain Morris and Damon Beesley

Iain Morris and Damon Beesley are the co-writers and co-creators of *The Inbetweeners*. They are also founders of Bwark Productions, the company producing the show.

Morris was born on 6 August 1973 in Surrey, England. After finishing school, he studied Theology at Bristol University and then began writing and trying to work his way into the comedy scene. His life in comedy began by working on radio station XFM alongside the comedian Jimmy Carr, and the pair would also work alongside each other on many of Carr's stand-up productions. Morris also went on to become script editor for another Channel 4 hit series *Peep Show*, which starred comedy duo David Mitchell and Robert Webb.

Damon Beesley was born in 1971 in England and, after A-Levels, he took a different path to Iain Morris by moving on to the Channel 4 morning show *The Big Breakfast* and working his way up through the channel.

The pair met while working on Channel 4's satirical

THE WRITERS AND THE CAST COLLECT THEIR COMEDY AWARD.

late-night comedy *The 11 O'Clock Show*, which was also the launch pad for other big British comedians including Ricky Gervais and Sacha Baron Cohen. They went on to become flatmates and formed a solid writing partnership, with most of the writing coming from anecdotes of their own personal failings and occasional triumphs while growing up. In fact, many of the storylines from *The Inbetweeners* have come from their own experiences, such as the skidding incident, receiving a bright-yellow car and writing 'I love you' to a girl on a driveway. Much of the reason why the show has proved so popular is down to the viewer being able to relate to the antics of one, if not all, of the teenage boys in the show and that stems from the writers' own experiences and similar upbringing in suburban England.

After *The 11 O'Clock Show*, in 2004, Beesley and Morris founded Bwark Productions and went on to produce many of Jimmy Carr's stand-up shows from 2005 to 2010, not to mention *The Inbetweeners'* episodes and the 2011 movie feature. In addition to writing for *The Inbetweeners*, the pair have also penned two episodes for the hit HBO series *Flight of the Conchords* – a series in which two band members from New Zealand try to make it big in America.

Did you know?

Iain Morris and Damon Beesley were the names of characters in the second series of Extras, a BBC comedy written by Ricky Gervais and Stephen Merchant. The characters were a producer and writer working for the BBC, who try to help Gervais's character (Andy Millman) launch a comedy series.

X is for...

XFM

Radio station XFM has been broadcasting in London since 1997 and in Manchester since 2006. The commercial station is most famous in London for playing alternative and indie music. In addition, the show's presenters have often been top alternative comedians plucked just before they are ripe. Past presenters include Ricky Gervais, Stephen Merchant and Karl Pilkington, Simon Pegg, Russell Brand, Adam & Joe, Zane Lowe and Dermot O'Leary.

In 2003, comedian Jimmy Carr presented a show on Sundays from 10am to 1pm. He was joined as co-presenter by his friend (and comedy writer of *The*

Inbetweeners) Iain Morris. In a 2010 interview on XFM with current presenter Dave Berry, Carr expressed his delight at being back at the station: 'We used to love coming in and playing a bit of indie pop – it was brilliant!' He also reminisced about their 10am Sunday show: 'Sunday mornings was fabulous – we were probably broadcasting to eight stores in Camden Market! We would start at 10am and our listeners wouldn't be up yet.'

It wasn't only Jimmy who found himself back at his old radio station, though: Iain Morris also went back to his old stomping ground in 2008 to talk about the first series of *The Inbetweeners*, along with James Buckley (Jay). During the show, Iain described how some of the stories came about, while James tried out some chat-up lines on listeners phoning in.

'Xmas Party': Series One, Episode Six

It's the final episode in the first series and Will McKenzie (as the only candidate) has been elected chairman of the school's first-ever Xmas Prom committee.

First on his agenda is looking smart, and so Will, Simon and Neil all go to hire a suit, along with Simon's dad and Jay – who already has a suit but probably nothing better to do that day! Much to his dad's disappointment, Simon doesn't opt to look for the suit his dad was wearing on the night he and Simon's mum first had sex.

The owner of the suit-hire shop chooses what can best be described as classic designs, including a red velvet jacket and matching dickie bow for Will and a purple velvet jacket and dickie bow for Simon: 'Very jazzy!' Thankfully, the pair see sense and decide to opt for something of their own choice, while Neil asks for 'something special, something to make me stand out'!

The Xmas Prom isn't just a big occasion for Will, though. Simon sees it as his big chance to impress Carli, Jay has been promised the spot as DJ, while Neil in a massive revelation decides he may be ready for a relationship – possibly with his favourite biology teacher, Miss Timbs. Thanks to Simon's involvement, the guys have a few perks, as Jay points out: 'If we control the beer vouchers, we control the birds – the *drunk* birds!'

Will's role as chairman gives him the perfect opportunity to get all geeky, drawing up committee meetings, agendas and roles for everyone involved, although Big John only seems interested in food arrangements.

Despite his enthusiasm, Mr Gilbert lays down a few ground rules: everyone will get two alcoholic-drink tokens (and no heavy petting!). Gilbert's rules are the least of Will's concerns after school bully Mark Donovan warns him that, if he sees him anywhere near Charlotte 'Big Jugs' Hinchcliffe, he'll rip his throat out! Despite this minor hiccup, preparations go well and, on the day of the prom, the school hall is decorated and the stage ready.

As Neil's only agenda for the night is to make a statement, he decides to do this through his outfit. Taking advice from an article he's read in a lads' mag, he hires an outfit that will make him stand out and that, apparently, is going to make him irresistible to the opposite sex: an all-in-one suit with glittery collar, flared legs and a tight crotch! Unsurprisingly, Jay disagrees that this Elvis throwback will get Neil the kind of attention he wants and instead makes a focal point of what he *wouldn't* want people to see: 'Your cock – it looks like an acorn!'

Despite the distractions from Neil and Will flapping about getting the school hall ready in time, the prom starts off as a success. The hall looks good, everyone's turned up and people are actually having a good time. Things start to look up for Neil, especially as his favourite biology teacher – Miss Timbs – turns up to the party. Neil has already revealed that he 'nearly knocked one out' during a lesson when she was teaching the class about the reproductive system, and so, with more than his drink allowance, he decides to start his famous body popping with his teacher.

While Neil attempts his best moves on Miss Timbs, Simon tries to find Carli. Having hatched a plan with Jay on the DJ decks, he decides it's finally his chance to tell her how he feels about her. Jay stops the music so Si can declare his love but his plans are foiled because everyone's attention is taken up by Neil, who decides to tell Miss Timbs he loves her (boner included!).

Things start to deteriorate for Will, too, as Donovan pins him up against the wall for talking to Charlotte. Thanks to his efforts in organising the prom, the other pupils stick up for him, though, and Donovan spares his throat. He decides this is the best moment to make his speech, which leaves the others to return to thinking he's a 'Briefcase Wanker'.

The evening ends with three of the Inbetweeners happy with how things went. Simon realises that maybe it was for the best that he didn't declare his love for Carli, Will feels a bit more popular after pulling off a good party and Jay reveals he got involved in some heavy petting behind the DJ decks. And even Neil doesn't feel quite so bad after being turned down by Miss Timbs!

Did you know?
The record collection used by Jay during his DJ session in this episode actually belonged to one of the show's crew and has actually been used for sets at parties.

y is for...

Yoda

Yoda is the utterly embarrassing impression performed by Will in Episode One of Series Two. It comes about when Will tries a little too hard to impress new girl Lauren on the geography field trip. As he comes out with the immortal words 'Feisty one, you are', it's met with the complete confusion it deserves: 'Oh, I thought you might have a problem or Asperger's disease – have you ever been tested for anything?' The impression fails to hit the mark on so many levels as Lauren takes more of an interest in Will's friend Simon. Lauren only ever features in this one episode of the show.

Lauren is played by Jayne Wisener, an actress from

Northern Ireland. Jayne's biggest role to date came in 2007 acting alongside Johnny Depp in the Tim Burton movie *Sweeney Todd: The Demon Barber of Fleet Street*. After *The Inbetweeners*, she had a recurring role in *Casualty* for five episodes, and her most recent part came in the 2011 film *Jane Eyre*.

YouTube

Blake Harrison (Neil) tweeted a great YouTube video to his girlfriend Kerry Ann Lynch of a mash-up of internet sensation Rebecca Black and the Inbetweeners. The video called 'Rebecca Black is a Bus Wanker' starts off with the YouTube hit 'Friday' by Black. As the video shows Black standing at the bus stop singing the 'Friday' song, it flips to a clip of Jay hanging out of Simon's yellow Fiat shouting, 'Bus Wankers!'

The hilarious video has been an online hit with fans of the show, having been viewed over 30,000 times! This is set to rise even further when the show starts hitting US screens.

Z is for...

Zane Lowe

BBC Radio 1 DJ Zane Lowe is from New Zealand and he presents a show from 7 to 9pm, Mondays to Thursdays. On Thursday, 14 January 2010, he invited the cast of *The Inbetweeners* to take over his show and play some of their favourite tunes. Only three out of the gang of four were present during the broadcast: Simon Bird (Will), Joe Thomas (Simon) and James Buckley (Jay). Unfortunately, Blake Harrison (Neil) was unavailable on the day as he was at home preparing for a filming commitment but he did join the other guys on the phone later on in the show.

Listeners were asked to text or tweet the show (using

Zane's familiar shout out: 'Who's on board?') with any comments on the series and questions for the lads. One listener asked Simon Bird to break out his Yoda impression via Twitter, while another avid fan asked for help with his geography homework, to which they gladly obliged. Along with helping students with their studies, Simon, Joe and James also asked the listeners to text in to tell them what their mums were up to, with some of the highlights being 'My mum is yelling at the dog for eating butter again', 'My mum is squeezing my blackheads' and the text 'My mum is knitting a monkey' prompted Simon Bird to ask if that was a euphemism.

Among the bands that the lads elected to play on their takeover show were Pixies, The Libertines, Sleeper, The Smiths, MGMT, Oasis, Buzzcocks, The XX, The Cribs and Kanye West.

glossary...

And finally, here's your comprehensive guide to some of *The Inbetweeners'* rudest, lewdest, funniest and most outlandish words and phrases:

Acorn Cock: Small acorn-shaped penis, visible through a tight pair of trousers.
Balls Deep: Deep, penetrative sex.
Bender Mobile: A car full of 'Benders' (see *Benders*, below).
Benders: Derogatory term for a group of homosexuals.
Blind Date Books: A book not for reading, but for performing sexual acts on.
Blob, The: Derogatory term for female menstruation.
Boner: An erection, often occurring in the most

inappropriate situations and commonly hidden by
crossed legs.

Briefcase Wanker: A wanker who carries a briefcase
to school.

Bullshitter: A person who often bends the truth.

Bumder: Cross between a '*Bummer*' and a '*Bender*'.

Bummer: Derogatory term for a homosexual.

Bus Wanker: A wanker who must rely on public
transport – Bus Wankers can be found at bus stops
around the world.

Captain Cockwash: The master of a seafaring vessel,
who in his spare time enjoys washing his shipmates.

Clunge: Slang term for female genitalia.

Clunge Mag: Porn magazine.

Cock Seekers: People searching for penis.

Dirty Protest: Shitting yourself in a public area.

Ectoplasm: Male ejaculate.

Flange: Slang term for female genitalia.

Frothing: Female ejaculate.

Gagging For It: Sexually aroused.

Gash: Slang term for female genitalia.

Gashorama: A situation when there's a lot of
'*Gash*' present.

Horn Bucket: A promiscuous girl.

Immac: (Jay): 'What girls use to get a nice, smooth
fanny.'

Juggasaurus Rex: Female with larger-than-average breasts.

Knob: Slang word for a penis; also used to describe a door handle.

Lezzer: A lesbian.

Lick the Tip: Act performed during oral sex.

Midweek Wank: Also known as a 'Wednesday Wank', this is something to look forward to on a weekend of no action.

MILF: Mum I'd Like to Fuck.

Muff Wagon: A small car filled with women.

Munched Off: Oral sex, often performed on fifteen rugby players at once!

No Problemo: That's not a problem.

Nosh: Oral sex.

O.A.Paedo: Someone who shows sexual feelings towards the elderly.

Painters: (Having the Painters In): Derogatory term for female menstruation.

Peperami: A red-raw penis; one that's been subjected to an extended period of masturbation.

Porking: To partake in sexual intercourse with a member of the same or opposite sex. Not to be mistaken for pork scratchings – the fatty bar snack.

Porn-Star Tits: Big and perfectly round breasts that can only be supported by specially made bras.

Quick Tug: Masturbation at pace.

Rapey: Used to describe a sentence overly explicit in its sexual nature.

Sleeping Beauty: Masturbation with a hand numb through lack of blood circulation.

Snatch: Slang term for female genitalia.

Soppy Bollocks: Unused testicles.

Spunk: Male ejaculate.

Spunk Mobile: A car after a night's session of very heavy petting.

Stalk-On: An erection.

Street Smarts: When a person underperforms academically but shows promise in everyday situations.

Tactical Wank: Pre-sex masturbation intended to make the male last longer during sex.

Three-Course Meal: Not the traditional restaurant affair, Jay's version consists of a 'blowy, shag and anal'.

Udders: A cow's tits.

Up to My Nuts in Guts: An abundance of sexual activity.

V-Plates: Sign that all virgins must display on their car.

Vage: A shortened term for a woman's vagina.

Visual Wank-Bank: The process of storing a sexually arousing situation for masturbation later that evening.

Wanker: A person who frequently masturbates.

X-Rated: The Inbetweeners.

Yves Saint La Ponce: Designer fashion label particularly popular with effeminate men.

Zinger Tower Meal: A large chicken sandwich, often consumed on dates.